2ⁿᵈ Grade Math Workbook

Jungle Publishin

Introduction

This is a math book suitable for 7 - 8 year olds (Grade 2 in the U.S. and Canada) looking to test out their math skills.

It can also be used by Grade 1 students wanting to get ahead and Grade 3 kids who want to maintain and refresh their knowledge.

The book is divided up into seven parts:

- Number and Place Value
- Addition and Subtraction
- Multiplication and Division
- Fractions
- Measurement
- Geometry
- Statistics

Some of the exercises are explained in more detail on page 5.

Answers are included at the back.

Good luck!

This book belongs to:

....

Table of Contents

Exercises Explained

Part-whole Models

Part-whole models require you to add the two 'part' numbers at the bottom to make the 'whole' number at the top. In the example the two parts, 7 + 4, would make the whole number of 11.

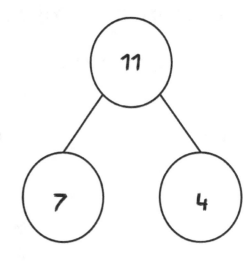

Table Drill

The table drill can be solved by multiplying the numbers from the left hand row with those in the top row.

×	12	1	0	9	4
12					
3					
5					
0					
1					

×	12	1	0	9	4
12	144	12	0	108	48
3	36	3	0	27	12
5	60	5	0	45	20
0	0	0	0	0	0
1	12	1	0	9	4

Fact Families

Fact families are groups of facts containing the same numbers.

Either two addition and two subtraction problems or two multiplication and two division problems will be given.

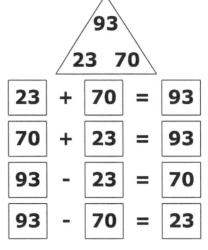

Section 1: Numbers and Place Value

Name: _____   Date: _____

Class: _____   Teacher: _____

Add the four numbers to the correct places on the line.

60, 35, 80, 25

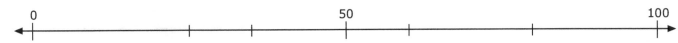

65, 25, 20, 90

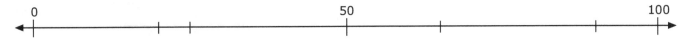

30, 55, 90, 10

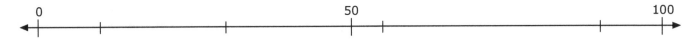

30, 70, 75, 90

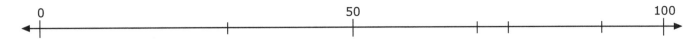

70, 15, 20, 35

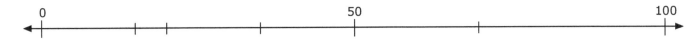

90, 35, 5, 40

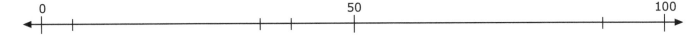

Counting on a Line

Do the same again. This time try without the guides!

35, 75, 60, 45

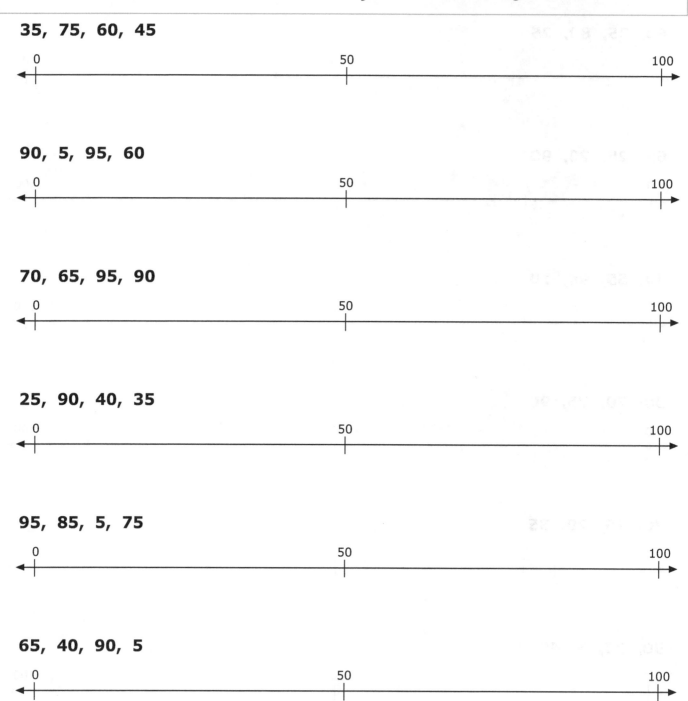

90, 5, 95, 60

70, 65, 95, 90

25, 90, 40, 35

95, 85, 5, 75

65, 40, 90, 5

Before and After

Add the numbers that come before and after those below.

Example: 16... 17... 18

1) .... **34** ....
2) .... **94** ....
3) .... **85** ....
4) .... **36** ....

5) .... **13** ....
6) .... **52** ....
7) .... **40** ....
8) .... **26** ....

9) .... **23** ....
10) .... **28** ....
11) .... **64** ....
12) .... **53** ....

13) .... **79** ....
14) .... **42** ....
15) .... **75** ....
16) .... **35** ....

Circle the Smallest Numbers

1) 67
81
6
86
93

2) 15
19
99
27
86

3) 18
23
57
61
65

4) 45
40
78
43
93

5) 93
52
21
67
40

6) 57
26
5
66
20

7) 63
56
58
13
72

8) 1
6
20
82
27

9) 74
83
3
16
43

10) 30
90
66
34
21

Score: _____ /26

9

Circle the Biggest Numbers

1)	2)	3)	4)	5)
46	15	89	61	39
65	60	13	64	19
23	38	32	43	95
9	45	7	89	16
22	36	23	63	10

6)	7)	8)	9)	10)
48	59	32	68	50
5	71	49	74	96
24	45	90	46	93
9	73	57	37	81
66	97	41	60	66

Circle the Smallest and Biggest Numbers

1)	2)	3)	4)	5)
3	86	32	89	92
99	52	85	71	73
36	71	26	91	23
0	49	15	41	0
73	92	68	8	67

6)	7)	8)	9)	10)
99	64	17	85	50
26	85	63	68	41
39	43	27	73	25
71	20	87	39	95
64	8	0	69	24

Score: /20

Circle the Odd Numbers

1)	2)	3)	4)	5)
73	76	12	41	8
10	35	99	5	64
4	33	84	94	54
17	74	27	60	6
29	60	47	71	5

6)	7)	8)	9)	10)
50	14	38	30	83
60	75	2	52	45
98	40	90	27	92
48	91	32	87	27
84	74	81	85	44

Circle the Even Numbers

1)	2)	3)	4)	5)
46	56	74	24	3
64	96	35	44	4
24	10	25	36	28
16	24	75	72	89
8	26	97	3	77

6)	7)	8)	9)	10)
11	68	51	91	27
27	70	23	65	51
20	3	82	5	89
21	38	18	6	61
4	50	42	95	39

Score: _____ /20

Numbers as Words

Write these numbers as words.

1) **17** ....

2) **11** ....

3) **12** ....

4) **15** ....

5) **16** ....

6) **6** ....

7) **13** ....

8) **19** ....

9) **9** ....

10) **5** ....

Score: /10

Words as Numbers

Write these words as numbers.

1) **sixteen**

2) **nineteen**

3) **twenty**

4) **eleven**

5) **six**

6) **seven**

7) **fifteen**

8) **eight**

9) **twelve**

10) **eighteen**

Score: /10

Place Values

Determine the place value of the underlined digit. For example: '3 ones', or '6 tens'.

1) **9̲8** = ...

2) **1̲** = ...

3) **2̲2** = ...

4) **4̲9** = ...

5) **1̲3** = ...

6) **37̲** = ...

7) **5̲** = ...

8) **4̲4** = ...

9) **5̲3** = ...

10) **6̲3** = ...

11) **4̲5** = ...

12) **2̲9** = ...

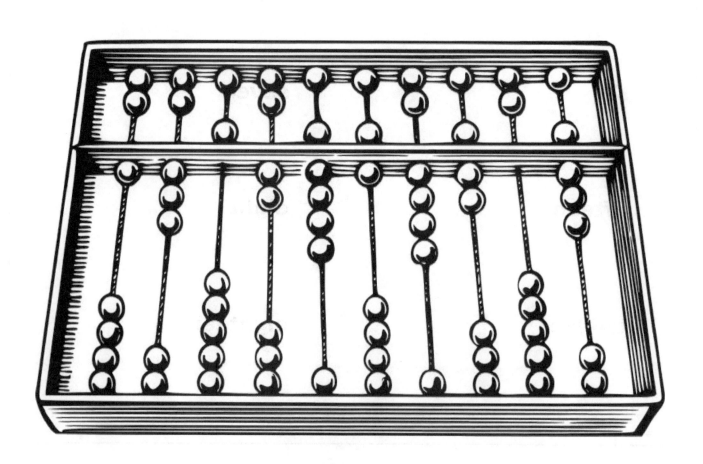

Number Comparison

Add > or < or =; Greater, less than or equal to (0-100).

1) 25 91   2) 1 65   3) 3 74   4) 21 6   5) 5 4

6) 18 2   7) 4 95   8) 42 1   9) 33 75   10) 5 5

Number Lines

Complete these number lines.

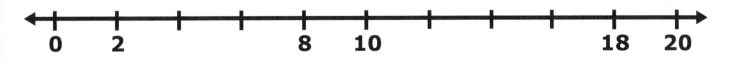

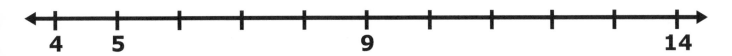

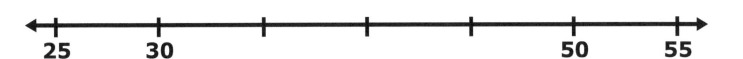

Order the Numbers

Order each set from lowest to highest (smallest number to biggest number).

1) 19 ....
    71 ....
    76 ....
    85 ....
    17 ....
    82 ....

2) 44 ....
    73 ....
    37 ....
    45 ....
    86 ....
    53 ....

3) 91 ....
    63 ....
    44 ....
    17 ....
    41 ....
    18 ....

Hint: Here we are counting in 2's, 3's, 5's and 10's.

1)

20		30	35				55		

2)

16	18			24				32	

3)

		69			60	57	54		

4)

	80	70	60						0

5)

	70		60	55				35	

6)

		15			30	35			50

7)

	20	30	40			70			

8)

82	80			74					64

9)

20		30	35				55		

10)

48		52			58	60			

Section 2: Addition and Subtraction

Name: _____ Date: _____

Class: _____ Teacher: _____

Pictorial Addition

Add these objects together. Draw them on!

1) ✾✾✾✾✾ ✾ + ✾✾✾✾✾ =

2) 🍁🍁🍁🍁🍁 🍁 + 🍁🍁🍁🍁🍁 🍁🍁 =

3) ✽✽✽✽✽ ✽✽✽✽ + ✽✽✽✽✽ ✽ =

4) ✸✸✸✸ + ✸✸✸✸ ✸✸ =

5) ♥♥♥♥♥ ♥♥ + ♥♥♥♥♥ ♥♥ =

Score: /5

Part-Whole Models

Fill out these part-whole models.

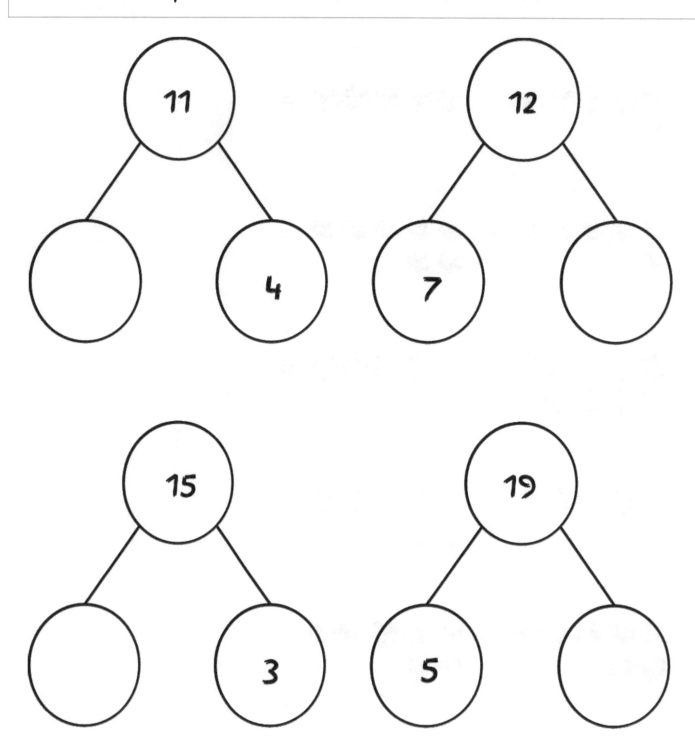

Adding Toucans

How many toucans can you see here?

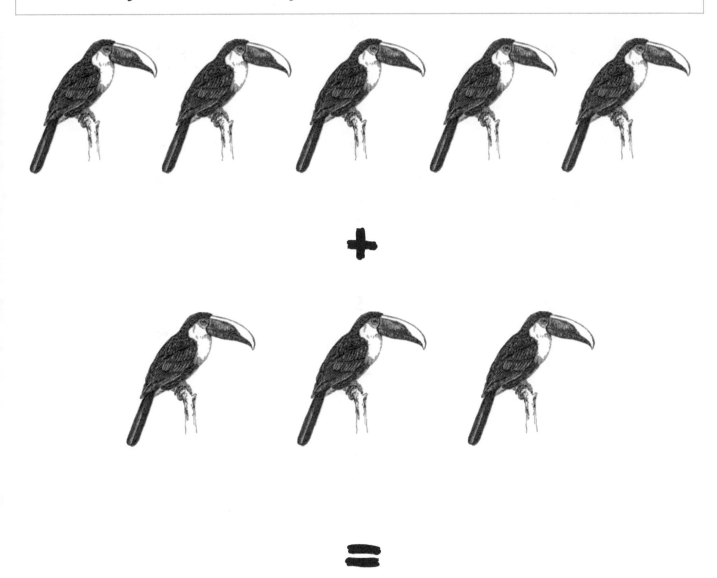

Adding 3 Single Digits

1)
```
    3
    1
+   2
_____
```

2)
```
    7
    9
+   5
_____
```

3)
```
    1
    3
+   4
_____
```

4)
```
    6
    2
+   7
_____
```

5)
```
    7
    4
+   8
_____
```

6)
```
    1
    6
+   9
_____
```

7)
```
    9
    5
+   8
_____
```

8)
```
    9
    4
+   8
_____
```

9)
```
    5
    4
+   5
_____
```

10)
```
    7
    2
+   4
_____
```

11)
```
    8
    5
+   6
_____
```

12)
```
    9
    6
+   9
_____
```

13)
```
    9
    8
+   5
_____
```

14)
```
    1
    7
+   3
_____
```

15)
```
    9
    6
+   4
_____
```

Score: _____ /15

Theater Tickets

Solve these theater problems.

1) James has six theater tickets and he wins four more. How many tickets does he have now?

2) He then gives 2 tickets to his friend El. How many is he left with now?

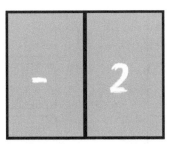

23

Fact Families: Addition and Subtraction

Complete these addition and subtraction families.

1)

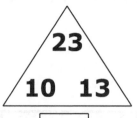

☐ + ☐ = ☐

☐ + ☐ = ☐

☐ - ☐ = ☐

☐ - ☐ = ☐

2)

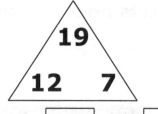

☐ + ☐ = ☐

☐ + ☐ = ☐

☐ - ☐ = ☐

☐ - ☐ = ☐

3)

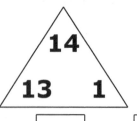

☐ + ☐ = ☐

☐ + ☐ = ☐

☐ - ☐ = ☐

☐ - ☐ = ☐

4)

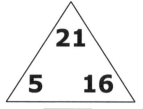

☐ + ☐ = ☐

☐ + ☐ = ☐

☐ - ☐ = ☐

☐ - ☐ = ☐

Score: /4

Written Questions

Solve these written questions.

a) What is 79 + 10?

_____

b) What does 8 tens + 3 ones equal?

_____

c) 20 - 5 + 10?

_____

d) What is the sum of 21 + 22?

_____

e) What is subtracted from 100 to make 75?

_____

f) 5 tens - 9 ones?

_____

Mixed Operations 0-20: Part 1

1) $4 - 2 =$ ....

2) $7 - 6 =$ ....

3) $12 - 4 =$ ....

4) $5 - 3 =$ ....

5) $14 + 4 =$ ....

6) $19 + 15 =$ ....

7) $2 + 9 =$ ....

8) $14 - 4 =$ ....

9) $14 + 1 =$ ....

10) $8 - 6 =$ ....

11) $8 + 12 =$ ....

12) $19 - 13 =$ ....

13) $4 + 6 =$ ....

14) $13 - 10 =$ ....

15) $14 + 2 =$ ....

16) $10 + 16 =$ ....

17) $6 + 5 =$ ....

18) $19 + 1 =$ ....

19) $14 - 8 =$ ....

20) $17 - 13 =$ ....

Score: /20

1)
$$4 + 5$$

2)
$$10 - 4$$

3)
$$5 - 3$$

4)
$$8 - 5$$

5)
$$9 - 4$$

6)
$$11 + 18$$

7)
$$4 + 14$$

8)
$$7 + 2$$

9)
$$5 + 9$$

10)
$$16 - 14$$

11)
$$17 - 0$$

12)
$$17 + 4$$

13)
$$12 + 6$$

14)
$$19 - 16$$

15)
$$11 - 2$$

16)
$$19 + 17$$

17)
$$7 - 0$$

18)
$$2 - 1$$

19)
$$12 - 6$$

20)
$$3 + 8$$

21)
$$15 + 5$$

22)
$$18 - 8$$

23)
$$2 + 12$$

24)
$$15 + 13$$

25)
$$9 + 18$$

26)
$$6 - 0$$

27)
$$12 + 5$$

28)
$$3 - 1$$

29)
$$14 - 13$$

30)
$$19 + 11$$

Score: /30

27

Charlie Croc!

Total the numbers from Charlie Crocodile's balloons.

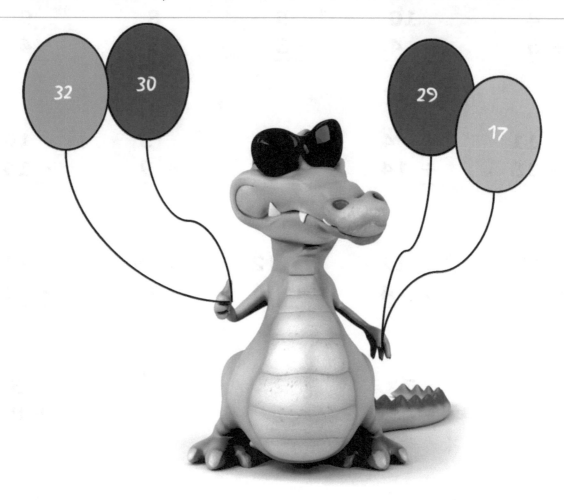

Left-hand side: **Right-hand side:**

_____   _____

Oops, the balloon on the far left has burst! Add the remaining three numbers.

_____

Adding Numbers 0-100: Part 1

Adding a multiple of ten to a double-digit number.

1) $16 + 40$

2) $41 + 30$

3) $21 + 50$

4) $19 + 30$

5) $6 + 20$

6) $7 + 50$

7) $17 + 40$

8) $9 + 30$

9) $41 + 20$

10) $41 + 10$

11) $17 + 20$

12) $6 + 50$

13) $44 + 50$

14) $12 + 60$

15) $15 + 60$

16) $32 + 50$

17) $49 + 30$

18) $11 + 40$

19) $11 + 20$

20) $13 + 60$

Score: /20

Adding Numbers 0-100: Part 2

Adding two double-digit numbers.

1)
$$41 + 12$$

2)
$$47 + 31$$

3)
$$48 + 27$$

4)
$$41 + 56$$

5)
$$48 + 35$$

6)
$$52 + 29$$

7)
$$60 + 22$$

8)
$$31 + 41$$

9)
$$64 + 21$$

10)
$$37 + 43$$

11)
$$31 + 62$$

12)
$$52 + 43$$

13)
$$53 + 46$$

14)
$$31 + 56$$

15)
$$42 + 46$$

16)
$$31 + 69$$

17)
$$40 + 42$$

18)
$$45 + 37$$

19)
$$51 + 41$$

20)
$$59 + 11$$

Score: ___ /20

Subtracting Numbers 0-100

Subtracting from a double-digit number.

1)
$$79 - 41$$

2)
$$61 - 6$$

3)
$$65 - 5$$

4)
$$56 - 25$$

5)
$$75 - 19$$

6)
$$80 - 11$$

7)
$$89 - 10$$

8)
$$58 - 5$$

9)
$$94 - 45$$

10)
$$60 - 35$$

11)
$$60 - 42$$

12)
$$99 - 32$$

13)
$$88 - 39$$

14)
$$81 - 31$$

15)
$$83 - 4$$

16)
$$82 - 15$$

17)
$$86 - 48$$

18)
$$65 - 28$$

19)
$$58 - 10$$

20)
$$79 - 16$$

Score: /20

Mixed Operations 0-100

1)   12
  + 21

2)   55
  + 44

3)   0
  + 24

4)   23
  − 12

5)   14
  + 32

6)   50
  − 39

7)   54
  − 30

8)   62
  − 28

9)   42
  − 5

10)   7
  − 4

11)   38
  − 7

12)   10
  + 36

13)   23
  + 3

14)   21
  + 17

15)   61
  − 33

16)   8
  − 6

17)   44
  − 10

18)   17
  − 9

19)   67
  − 29

20)   9
  − 4

21)   56
  − 23

22)   22
  − 19

23)   33
  + 9

24)   14
  + 56

25)   30
  + 1

26)   44
  + 1

27)   14
  + 31

28)   1
  + 42

29)   7
  + 21

30)   10
  + 47

Score: /30

Section 3: Multiplication and Division

Name: _____ Date: _____

Class: _____ Teacher: _____

Multiplying by 2: Part 1

1)
   8
× 2

2)
   7
× 2

3)
   5
× 2

4)
   2
× 2

5)
   6
× 2

6)
   3
× 2

7)
   9
× 2

8)
   1
× 2

9)
   4
× 2

10)
   7
× 2

11)
   1
× 2

12)
   8
× 2

13)
   7
× 2

14)
   2
× 2

15)
   7
× 2

16)
   6
× 2

17)
   6
× 2

18)
   3
× 2

19)
   5
× 2

20)
   3
× 2

21)
   8
× 2

22)
   7
× 2

23)
   7
× 2

24)
   6
× 2

25)
   2
× 2

26)
   6
× 2

27)
   4
× 2

28)
   5
× 2

29)
   5
× 2

30)
   2
× 2

Score: /30

Multiplying by 2: Part 2

1)
$$\begin{array}{r} 2 \\ \times\ 5 \\ \hline \end{array}$$

2)
$$\begin{array}{r} 2 \\ \times\ 3 \\ \hline \end{array}$$

3)
$$\begin{array}{r} 2 \\ \times\ 4 \\ \hline \end{array}$$

4)
$$\begin{array}{r} 2 \\ \times\ 8 \\ \hline \end{array}$$

5)
$$\begin{array}{r} 2 \\ \times\ 9 \\ \hline \end{array}$$

6)
$$\begin{array}{r} 2 \\ \times\ 7 \\ \hline \end{array}$$

7)
$$\begin{array}{r} 2 \\ \times\ 2 \\ \hline \end{array}$$

8)
$$\begin{array}{r} 2 \\ \times\ 6 \\ \hline \end{array}$$

9)
$$\begin{array}{r} 2 \\ \times\ 1 \\ \hline \end{array}$$

10)
$$\begin{array}{r} 2 \\ \times\ 4 \\ \hline \end{array}$$

11)
$$\begin{array}{r} 2 \\ \times\ 7 \\ \hline \end{array}$$

12)
$$\begin{array}{r} 2 \\ \times\ 9 \\ \hline \end{array}$$

13)
$$\begin{array}{r} 2 \\ \times\ 6 \\ \hline \end{array}$$

14)
$$\begin{array}{r} 2 \\ \times\ 6 \\ \hline \end{array}$$

15)
$$\begin{array}{r} 2 \\ \times\ 2 \\ \hline \end{array}$$

16)
$$\begin{array}{r} 2 \\ \times\ 3 \\ \hline \end{array}$$

17)
$$\begin{array}{r} 2 \\ \times\ 1 \\ \hline \end{array}$$

18)
$$\begin{array}{r} 2 \\ \times\ 8 \\ \hline \end{array}$$

19)
$$\begin{array}{r} 2 \\ \times\ 6 \\ \hline \end{array}$$

20)
$$\begin{array}{r} 2 \\ \times\ 7 \\ \hline \end{array}$$

21)
$$\begin{array}{r} 2 \\ \times\ 5 \\ \hline \end{array}$$

22)
$$\begin{array}{r} 2 \\ \times\ 2 \\ \hline \end{array}$$

23)
$$\begin{array}{r} 2 \\ \times\ 3 \\ \hline \end{array}$$

24)
$$\begin{array}{r} 2 \\ \times\ 7 \\ \hline \end{array}$$

25)
$$\begin{array}{r} 2 \\ \times\ 6 \\ \hline \end{array}$$

26)
$$\begin{array}{r} 2 \\ \times\ 7 \\ \hline \end{array}$$

27)
$$\begin{array}{r} 2 \\ \times\ 1 \\ \hline \end{array}$$

28)
$$\begin{array}{r} 2 \\ \times\ 1 \\ \hline \end{array}$$

29)
$$\begin{array}{r} 2 \\ \times\ 1 \\ \hline \end{array}$$

30)
$$\begin{array}{r} 2 \\ \times\ 4 \\ \hline \end{array}$$

Score: /30

Multiplying by 5: Part 1

1) 5 × 5

2) 1 × 5

3) 8 × 5

4) 6 × 5

5) 9 × 5

6) 3 × 5

7) 7 × 5

8) 4 × 5

9) 2 × 5

10) 3 × 5

11) 5 × 5

12) 5 × 5

13) 2 × 5

14) 3 × 5

15) 6 × 5

16) 8 × 5

17) 4 × 5

18) 6 × 5

19) 6 × 5

20) 3 × 5

21) 9 × 5

22) 9 × 5

23) 9 × 5

24) 2 × 5

25) 3 × 5

26) 3 × 5

27) 7 × 5

28) 4 × 5

29) 4 × 5

30) 7 × 5

Score: /30

Multiplying by 5: Part 2

1) 5×1

2) 5×6

3) 5×2

4) 5×5

5) 5×7

6) 5×3

7) 5×8

8) 5×4

9) 5×9

10) 5×1

11) 5×6

12) 5×3

13) 5×3

14) 5×2

15) 5×1

16) 5×5

17) 5×2

18) 5×5

19) 5×3

20) 5×9

21) 5×7

22) 5×8

23) 5×1

24) 5×9

25) 5×5

26) 5×2

27) 5×3

28) 5×3

29) 5×6

30) 5×5

Score: /30

1) $\begin{array}{r} 8 \\ \times\ 10 \\ \hline \end{array}$
2) $\begin{array}{r} 1 \\ \times\ 10 \\ \hline \end{array}$
3) $\begin{array}{r} 6 \\ \times\ 10 \\ \hline \end{array}$
4) $\begin{array}{r} 7 \\ \times\ 10 \\ \hline \end{array}$
5) $\begin{array}{r} 3 \\ \times\ 10 \\ \hline \end{array}$

6) $\begin{array}{r} 4 \\ \times\ 10 \\ \hline \end{array}$
7) $\begin{array}{r} 9 \\ \times\ 10 \\ \hline \end{array}$
8) $\begin{array}{r} 5 \\ \times\ 10 \\ \hline \end{array}$
9) $\begin{array}{r} 2 \\ \times\ 10 \\ \hline \end{array}$
10) $\begin{array}{r} 6 \\ \times\ 10 \\ \hline \end{array}$

11) $\begin{array}{r} 7 \\ \times\ 10 \\ \hline \end{array}$
12) $\begin{array}{r} 7 \\ \times\ 10 \\ \hline \end{array}$
13) $\begin{array}{r} 3 \\ \times\ 10 \\ \hline \end{array}$
14) $\begin{array}{r} 9 \\ \times\ 10 \\ \hline \end{array}$
15) $\begin{array}{r} 5 \\ \times\ 10 \\ \hline \end{array}$

16) $\begin{array}{r} 5 \\ \times\ 10 \\ \hline \end{array}$
17) $\begin{array}{r} 2 \\ \times\ 10 \\ \hline \end{array}$
18) $\begin{array}{r} 4 \\ \times\ 10 \\ \hline \end{array}$
19) $\begin{array}{r} 3 \\ \times\ 10 \\ \hline \end{array}$
20) $\begin{array}{r} 1 \\ \times\ 10 \\ \hline \end{array}$

21) $\begin{array}{r} 8 \\ \times\ 10 \\ \hline \end{array}$
22) $\begin{array}{r} 2 \\ \times\ 10 \\ \hline \end{array}$
23) $\begin{array}{r} 6 \\ \times\ 10 \\ \hline \end{array}$
24) $\begin{array}{r} 3 \\ \times\ 10 \\ \hline \end{array}$
25) $\begin{array}{r} 2 \\ \times\ 10 \\ \hline \end{array}$

26) $\begin{array}{r} 8 \\ \times\ 10 \\ \hline \end{array}$
27) $\begin{array}{r} 6 \\ \times\ 10 \\ \hline \end{array}$
28) $\begin{array}{r} 5 \\ \times\ 10 \\ \hline \end{array}$
29) $\begin{array}{r} 4 \\ \times\ 10 \\ \hline \end{array}$
30) $\begin{array}{r} 5 \\ \times\ 10 \\ \hline \end{array}$

Score: /30

Multiplying by 10: Part 2

1) $\begin{array}{r} 10 \\ \times\ 8 \\ \hline \end{array}$
2) $\begin{array}{r} 10 \\ \times\ 7 \\ \hline \end{array}$
3) $\begin{array}{r} 10 \\ \times\ 2 \\ \hline \end{array}$
4) $\begin{array}{r} 10 \\ \times\ 6 \\ \hline \end{array}$
5) $\begin{array}{r} 10 \\ \times\ 5 \\ \hline \end{array}$

6) $\begin{array}{r} 10 \\ \times\ 4 \\ \hline \end{array}$
7) $\begin{array}{r} 10 \\ \times\ 9 \\ \hline \end{array}$
8) $\begin{array}{r} 10 \\ \times\ 3 \\ \hline \end{array}$
9) $\begin{array}{r} 10 \\ \times\ 1 \\ \hline \end{array}$
10) $\begin{array}{r} 10 \\ \times\ 5 \\ \hline \end{array}$

11) $\begin{array}{r} 10 \\ \times\ 6 \\ \hline \end{array}$
12) $\begin{array}{r} 10 \\ \times\ 3 \\ \hline \end{array}$
13) $\begin{array}{r} 10 \\ \times\ 2 \\ \hline \end{array}$
14) $\begin{array}{r} 10 \\ \times\ 7 \\ \hline \end{array}$
15) $\begin{array}{r} 10 \\ \times\ 2 \\ \hline \end{array}$

16) $\begin{array}{r} 10 \\ \times\ 7 \\ \hline \end{array}$
17) $\begin{array}{r} 10 \\ \times\ 4 \\ \hline \end{array}$
18) $\begin{array}{r} 10 \\ \times\ 3 \\ \hline \end{array}$
19) $\begin{array}{r} 10 \\ \times\ 3 \\ \hline \end{array}$
20) $\begin{array}{r} 10 \\ \times\ 7 \\ \hline \end{array}$

21) $\begin{array}{r} 10 \\ \times\ 7 \\ \hline \end{array}$
22) $\begin{array}{r} 10 \\ \times\ 5 \\ \hline \end{array}$
23) $\begin{array}{r} 10 \\ \times\ 2 \\ \hline \end{array}$
24) $\begin{array}{r} 10 \\ \times\ 2 \\ \hline \end{array}$
25) $\begin{array}{r} 10 \\ \times\ 5 \\ \hline \end{array}$

26) $\begin{array}{r} 10 \\ \times\ 8 \\ \hline \end{array}$
27) $\begin{array}{r} 10 \\ \times\ 7 \\ \hline \end{array}$
28) $\begin{array}{r} 10 \\ \times\ 5 \\ \hline \end{array}$
29) $\begin{array}{r} 10 \\ \times\ 8 \\ \hline \end{array}$
30) $\begin{array}{r} 10 \\ \times\ 4 \\ \hline \end{array}$

Score: /30

Right or wrong?

This table has 4 incorrect sums. Highlight the wrong ones!

2 x 1 = 4	2 x 4 = 8	3 x 6 = 18
2 x 2 = 4	5 ÷ 4 = 12	4 x 5 = 20
100 ÷ 10 = 1	3 x 3 = 9	2 x 4 = 8
2 x 1 = 2	3 x 4 = 12	2 ÷ 2 = 2

Multiplication Patterns

Fill in the empty spaces starting from zero.

1) **Count by 12 from 0 to 108**

0				48		72			

2) **Count by 1 from 0 to 9**

		2	3						9

3) **Count by 6 from 0 to 54**

		12				36		48	

4) **Count by 8 from 0 to 72**

0		16						64	

5) **Count by 7 from 0 to 63**

0				28		42			

6) **Count by 4 from 0 to 36**

		8	12						36

7) **Count by 5 from 0 to 45**

						30	35	40	

8) **Count by 11 from 0 to 99**

					55		77		99

Score: 18

Word Problems: Multiplication

Solve these multiplication word problems.

1) Amy has two times more pears than Steven. Steven has three pears. How many pears does Amy have?

2) Jake swims three laps every day. How many laps will Jake swim in four days?

3) Paul can cycle two miles per hour. How far can Paul cycle in one hours?

4) Sarah's garden has four rows of pumpkins. Each row has four pumpkins. How many pumpkins does Sarah have in all?

5) If there are six apples in each box and there is one boxes, how many apples are there in total?

Score: /5

Dividing by 2

1) $56 \div 2 =$ _____

2) $80 \div 2 =$ _____

3) $50 \div 2 =$ _____

4) $14 \div 2 =$ _____

5) $36 \div 2 =$ _____

6) $78 \div 2 =$ _____

7) $92 \div 2 =$ _____

8) $10 \div 2 =$ _____

9) $96 \div 2 =$ _____

10) $4 \div 2 =$ _____

11) $12 \div 2 =$ _____

12) $100 \div 2 =$ _____

13) $76 \div 2 =$ _____

14) $38 \div 2 =$ _____

15) $72 \div 2 =$ _____

16) $26 \div 2 =$ _____

17) $34 \div 2 =$ _____

18) $52 \div 2 =$ _____

19) $74 \div 2 =$ _____

20) $18 \div 2 =$ _____

21) $28 \div 2 =$ _____

22) $68 \div 2 =$ _____

23) $84 \div 2 =$ _____

24) $86 \div 2 =$ _____

25) $32 \div 2 =$ _____

26) $24 \div 2 =$ _____

27) $16 \div 2 =$ _____

28) $46 \div 2 =$ _____

29) $20 \div 2 =$ _____

30) $30 \div 2 =$ _____

Score: _____ /30

Dividing by 5

1) $40 \div 5 =$ _____

2) $45 \div 5 =$ _____

3) $80 \div 5 =$ _____

4) $10 \div 5 =$ _____

5) $55 \div 5 =$ _____

6) $15 \div 5 =$ _____

7) $50 \div 5 =$ _____

8) $25 \div 5 =$ _____

9) $100 \div 5 =$ _____

10) $30 \div 5 =$ _____

11) $85 \div 5 =$ _____

12) $60 \div 5 =$ _____

13) $20 \div 5 =$ _____

14) $5 \div 5 =$ _____

15) $70 \div 5 =$ _____

16) $75 \div 5 =$ _____

17) $65 \div 5 =$ _____

18) $95 \div 5 =$ _____

19) $35 \div 5 =$ _____

20) $90 \div 5 =$ _____

21) $95 \div 5 =$ _____

22) $25 \div 5 =$ _____

23) $30 \div 5 =$ _____

24) $20 \div 5 =$ _____

25) $5 \div 5 =$ _____

26) $55 \div 5 =$ _____

27) $50 \div 5 =$ _____

28) $40 \div 5 =$ _____

29) $40 \div 5 =$ _____

30) $65 \div 5 =$ _____

Score: /30

Dividing by 10

1) $90 \div 10 = $ _____

2) $50 \div 10 = $ _____

3) $40 \div 10 = $ _____

4) $60 \div 10 = $ _____

5) $20 \div 10 = $ _____

6) $10 \div 10 = $ _____

7) $80 \div 10 = $ _____

8) $70 \div 10 = $ _____

9) $100 \div 10 = $ _____

10) $30 \div 10 = $ _____

11) $80 \div 10 = $ _____

12) $80 \div 10 = $ _____

13) $100 \div 10 = $ _____

14) $30 \div 10 = $ _____

15) $80 \div 10 = $ _____

16) $70 \div 10 = $ _____

17) $20 \div 10 = $ _____

18) $60 \div 10 = $ _____

19) $70 \div 10 = $ _____

20) $40 \div 10 = $ _____

Score: _____ /20

Word Problems: Division

Solve these division word problems.

1) Alice made 18 cookies for a bake sale. She put the cookies in bags, with nine cookies in each bag. How many bags did she have for the bake sale?

2) How many nine cm pieces of rope can you cut from a rope that is 36 cm long?

3) Sandra ordered five pizzas. The bill for the pizzas came to $25. What was the cost of each pizza?

4) You have 30 balls and want to share them equally with six people. How many balls would each person get?

5) David is reading a book with 27 pages. If David wants to read the same number of pages every day, how many pages would David have to read each day to finish in nine days?

Score: _____ /5

Table Drill

Complete these multiplication tables.

1)

×	10	7	11	8	5
8					
10					
3	30	21			
7					
0					

2)

×	3	1	9	8	5
1					
4					
3		3	27		
5					
11					

3)

×	4	12	7	2	11
7					
10					
3					
5			35	10	
0					

4)

×	8	3	12	6	7
10					
5					
12					
4					28
3			36		

Score: _____ /4

Fact Families: Multiplication and Division

Complete these multiplication and division families.

1)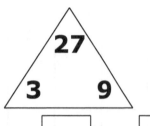

$\square$ × $\square$ = $\square$

$\square$ × $\square$ = $\square$

$\square$ ÷ $\square$ = $\square$

$\square$ ÷ $\square$ = $\square$

2)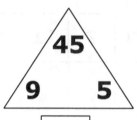

$\square$ × $\square$ = $\square$

$\square$ × $\square$ = $\square$

$\square$ ÷ $\square$ = $\square$

$\square$ ÷ $\square$ = $\square$

3)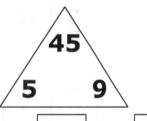

$\square$ × $\square$ = $\square$

$\square$ × $\square$ = $\square$

$\square$ ÷ $\square$ = $\square$

$\square$ ÷ $\square$ = $\square$

4)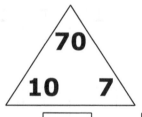

$\square$ × $\square$ = $\square$

$\square$ × $\square$ = $\square$

$\square$ ÷ $\square$ = $\square$

$\square$ ÷ $\square$ = $\square$

Score: /4

The Maze!

Answer these sums and help Charlie through the maze!

7 X 1 =

8 ÷ 2 =

8 X 10 =

14 ÷ 7 =

7 X 9 =

7 X 4 =

3 X 8 =

5 X 8 =

Section 4: Fractions

Name: _____   Date: _____

Class: _____   Teacher: _____

Shading Shapes

Shade in half of each shape.

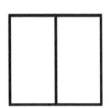   

a) How many separate halves are there on these four shapes?

b) Shade in 1/4 of each shape. Choose a different method each time.

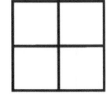 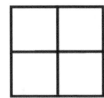 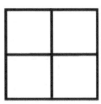

c) Shade in 3/4 of each shape. Choose a different method each time.

 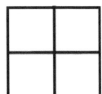 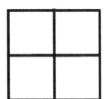

Shade the Fraction

Shade the rectangles as per the fraction provided.

1) $\dfrac{2}{5}$ =

2) $\dfrac{2}{3}$ =

3) $\dfrac{1}{5}$ =

4) $\dfrac{1}{2}$ =

5) $\dfrac{3}{8}$ =

6) $\dfrac{1}{3}$ =

7) $\dfrac{2}{6}$ =

8) $\dfrac{3}{4}$ =

9) $\dfrac{4}{6}$ =

10) $\dfrac{5}{8}$ =

Score: /10

Identify the Shaded Fraction

Identify the fraction as per the shaded rectangles.

1)  =

2)  =

3)  =

4) =

5) =

6) =

7) =

8) =

9) =

10) =

Score: /10

Draw a line to the fraction of the pizza Charlie has eaten.

$$\frac{1}{2} \qquad \frac{1}{3} \qquad \frac{1}{4} \qquad \frac{1}{5} \qquad \frac{2}{3} \qquad \frac{3}{4}$$

Charlie eats another 1/2 of the pizza. How much is left now?

Write the fraction in the appropriate place.

1) $1\dfrac{1}{4}$ $1\dfrac{3}{4}$ $\dfrac{3}{4}$ $\dfrac{1}{4}$

```
0                              1                              2
├──┼──┼──┼──┼──┼──┼──┤
```

2) $\dfrac{3}{4}$ $1\dfrac{1}{2}$ $1\dfrac{1}{4}$ $\dfrac{1}{2}$

```
0                              1                              2
├──┼──┼──┼──┼──┼──┼──┤
```

3) $\dfrac{3}{4}$ $1\dfrac{1}{2}$ $\dfrac{1}{2}$ $\dfrac{1}{4}$

```
0                              1                              2
├──┼──┼──┼──┼──┼──┼──┤
```

4) $\dfrac{1}{4}$ $1\dfrac{3}{4}$ $1\dfrac{1}{4}$ $\dfrac{3}{4}$

```
0                              1                              2
├──┼──┼──┼──┼──┼──┼──┤
```

Score: _____ /4

Add the Fractions

Find the sum of the two fractions.

1)
$$+ \frac{\frac{2}{4}}{\frac{3}{4}}$$

2)
$$+ \frac{\frac{1}{3}}{\frac{2}{3}}$$

3)
$$+ \frac{\frac{4}{5}}{\frac{4}{5}}$$

4)
$$+ \frac{\frac{4}{6}}{\frac{1}{6}}$$

5)
$$+ \frac{\frac{1}{2}}{\frac{1}{2}}$$

6)
$$+ \frac{\frac{2}{4}}{\frac{1}{4}}$$

7)
$$+ \frac{\frac{2}{5}}{\frac{4}{5}}$$

8)
$$+ \frac{\frac{2}{3}}{\frac{2}{3}}$$

9)
$$+ \frac{\frac{1}{4}}{\frac{1}{4}}$$

10)
$$+ \frac{\frac{2}{3}}{\frac{1}{3}}$$

11)
$$+ \frac{\frac{2}{5}}{\frac{3}{5}}$$

12)
$$+ \frac{\frac{1}{6}}{\frac{1}{6}}$$

13)
$$+ \frac{\frac{3}{4}}{\frac{1}{4}}$$

14)
$$+ \frac{\frac{3}{6}}{\frac{1}{6}}$$

15)
$$+ \frac{\frac{3}{5}}{\frac{4}{5}}$$

16)
$$+ \frac{\frac{3}{6}}{\frac{5}{6}}$$

17)
$$+ \frac{\frac{2}{5}}{\frac{1}{5}}$$

18)
$$+ \frac{\frac{4}{5}}{\frac{3}{5}}$$

19)
$$+ \frac{\frac{5}{6}}{\frac{1}{6}}$$

20)
$$+ \frac{\frac{1}{5}}{\frac{4}{5}}$$

Score: /20

Split the animals into equal groups.

There are _____ sets of _____ rhinos.

How many ways can you split the elephants into equal parts?

Simplifying Fractions

Simplify these fractions to their lowest common denominators.

1) $\dfrac{16}{32} =$

2) $\dfrac{40}{48} =$

3) $\dfrac{18}{27} =$

4) $\dfrac{24}{32} =$

5) $\dfrac{15}{25} =$

6) $\dfrac{28}{35} =$

7) $\dfrac{54}{72} =$

8) $\dfrac{7}{28} =$

9) $\dfrac{9}{27} =$

10) $\dfrac{20}{24} =$

11) $\dfrac{42}{48} =$

12) $\dfrac{36}{45} =$

13) $\dfrac{6}{18} =$

14) $\dfrac{25}{30} =$

15) $\dfrac{9}{12} =$

16) $\dfrac{27}{54} =$

17) $\dfrac{49}{56} =$

18) $\dfrac{12}{15} =$

19) $\dfrac{7}{21} =$

20) $\dfrac{5}{20} =$

Score: /20

Equivalent Fractions

Complete the equivalent fractions.

1) $\dfrac{}{4} = \dfrac{8}{32}$ 2) $\dfrac{}{3} = \dfrac{6}{18}$ 3) $\dfrac{1}{4} = \dfrac{}{20}$ 4) $\dfrac{}{3} = \dfrac{8}{12}$

5) $\dfrac{3}{4} = \dfrac{}{8}$ 6) $\dfrac{1}{3} = \dfrac{}{6}$ 7) $\dfrac{3}{4} = \dfrac{}{12}$ 8) $\dfrac{1}{3} = \dfrac{}{21}$

9) $\dfrac{}{4} = \dfrac{20}{40}$ 10) $\dfrac{}{3} = \dfrac{9}{27}$ 11) $\dfrac{1}{4} = \dfrac{}{16}$ 12) $\dfrac{3}{4} = \dfrac{}{36}$

13) $\dfrac{2}{3} = \dfrac{}{30}$ 14) $\dfrac{}{4} = \dfrac{10}{20}$ 15) $\dfrac{}{4} = \dfrac{4}{8}$ 16) $\dfrac{}{3} = \dfrac{14}{21}$

17) $\dfrac{2}{4} = \dfrac{}{36}$ 18) $\dfrac{}{4} = \dfrac{6}{24}$ 19) $\dfrac{}{4} = \dfrac{16}{32}$ 20) $\dfrac{}{4} = \dfrac{3}{12}$

Score: _____ /20

Comparing Fractions

Compare the numbers. Add: > or < or =

1) $\frac{2}{8}$ ___ $\frac{3}{4}$

2) $\frac{2}{3}$ ___ $\frac{3}{6}$

3) $\frac{1}{5}$ ___ $\frac{2}{4}$

4) $\frac{7}{8}$ ___ $\frac{2}{3}$

5) $\frac{2}{4}$ ___ $\frac{3}{8}$

6) $\frac{1}{3}$ ___ $\frac{3}{5}$

7) $\frac{3}{6}$ ___ $\frac{4}{8}$

8) $\frac{2}{4}$ ___ $\frac{2}{3}$

9) $\frac{2}{5}$ ___ $\frac{5}{6}$

10) $\frac{1}{3}$ ___ $\frac{5}{6}$

11) $\frac{2}{5}$ ___ $\frac{5}{8}$

12) $\frac{1}{4}$ ___ $\frac{3}{8}$

13) $\frac{3}{4}$ ___ $\frac{1}{3}$

14) $\frac{5}{6}$ ___ $\frac{2}{5}$

15) $\frac{4}{5}$ ___ $\frac{1}{6}$

16) $\frac{1}{8}$ ___ $\frac{2}{3}$

17) $\frac{2}{4}$ ___ $\frac{3}{6}$

18) $\frac{1}{5}$ ___ $\frac{1}{3}$

19) $\frac{6}{8}$ ___ $\frac{1}{4}$

20) $\frac{1}{4}$ ___ $\frac{3}{6}$

Score: _____ /20

Shade the Fraction

Shade the blocks as per the fraction provided.

1) 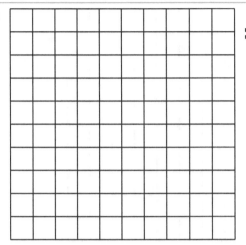 $= \dfrac{3}{5}$

2) 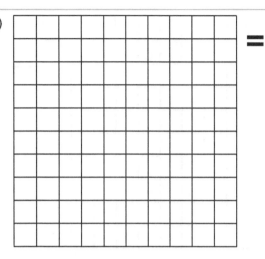 $= \dfrac{9}{10}$

3) 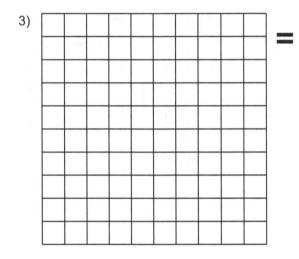 $= \dfrac{1}{2}$

4) 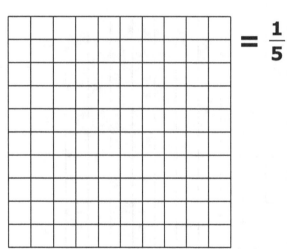 $= \dfrac{1}{5}$

5) 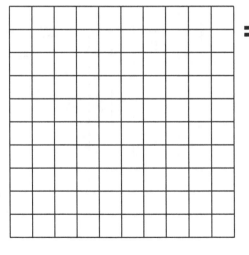 $= \dfrac{1}{10}$

6) 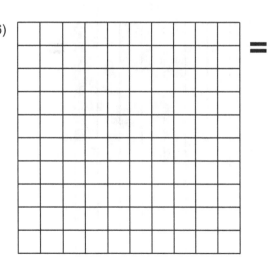 $= \dfrac{4}{5}$

Identify the Shaded Fraction

Write the fraction using the lowest common denominator.

1) 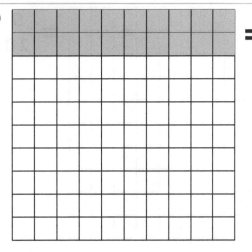 = ____

2) 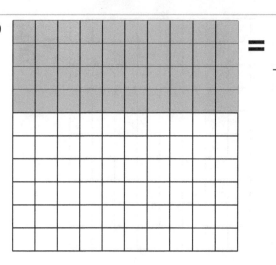 = ____

3) 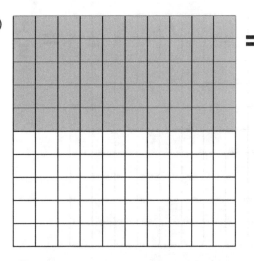 = ____

4) 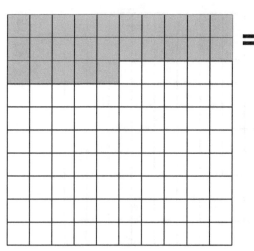 = ____

5) 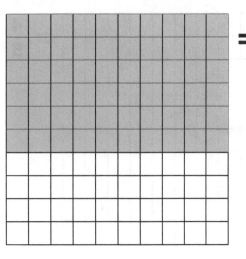 = ____

6) 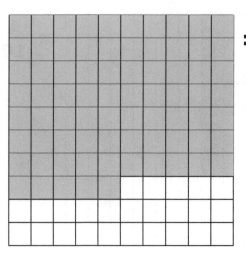 = ____

Translating Fractions to Whole Numbers

Write in the numbers that are equal to these fractions.

1) $\frac{1}{3}$ of 9 =

2) $\frac{6}{10}$ of 10 =

3) $\frac{3}{8}$ of 8 =

4) $\frac{4}{5}$ of 5 =

5) $\frac{3}{4}$ of 4 =

6) $\frac{6}{8}$ of 8 =

7) $\frac{3}{10}$ of 10 =

8) $\frac{3}{6}$ of 6 =

9) $\frac{1}{2}$ of 8 =

10) $\frac{17}{20}$ of 20 =

11) $\frac{2}{3}$ of 6 =

12) $\frac{1}{2}$ of 6 =

13) $\frac{2}{4}$ of 4 =

14) $\frac{5}{6}$ of 6 =

15) $\frac{1}{10}$ of 10 =

16) $\frac{2}{5}$ of 5 =

17) $\frac{13}{20}$ of 20 =

18) $\frac{5}{8}$ of 8 =

19) $\frac{1}{3}$ of 3 =

20) $\frac{2}{6}$ of 6 =

Score: _____ /20

Section 5: Measurement

Name: _____   Date: _____

Class: _____   Teacher: _____

Measuring Lines

1)

_____

2)

_____

3)

_____

4)

_____

5)

_____

6)

_____

7)

_____

8)

_____

9)

_____

10)

_____

a) Measure the lines. Which line is the longest, and which is the shortest?

_____

b) How much longer (in cm) is the longest line than the shortest?

_____

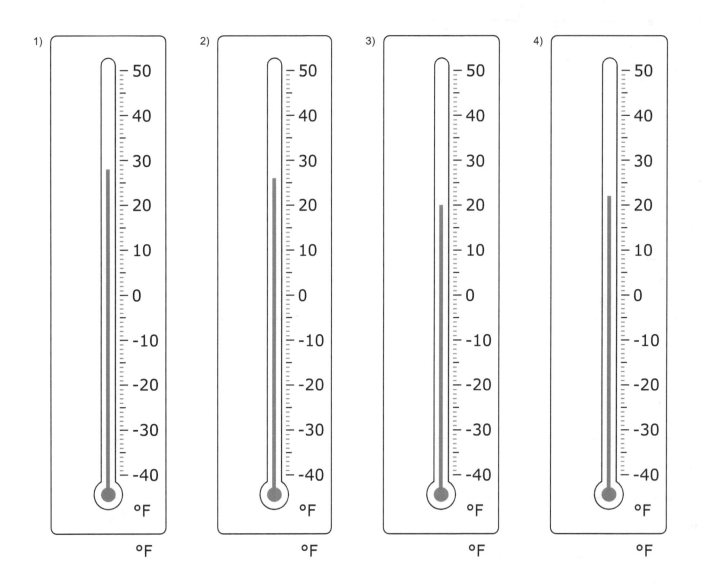

1) °F

2) °F

3) °F

4) °F

a) Write in the temperatures for all the thermometers.

b) Which thermometer is hottest and which is the coolest?

Gauge the Heat!

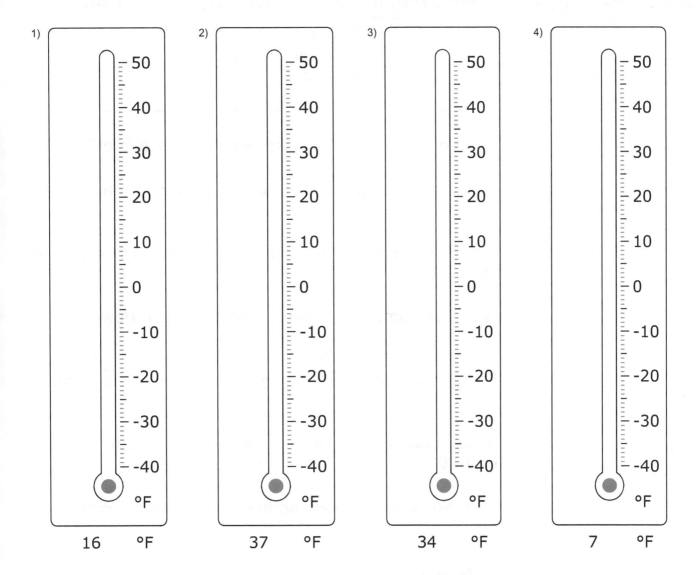

1) 16 °F

2) 37 °F

3) 34 °F

4) 7 °F

a) Shade the thermometers with their correct temperatures.

b) Which thermometer is the hottest and by how much?

_____

c) The hottest thermometer rises by 13°F. How hot is it now?

_____

Shopping Problems

Solve these shopping problems. The answer bank shows all possible answers.

Hot dog = $1.30
Chips = $1.30
Hamburger = $2.50
Cheeseburger = $3.40

Cola = $1.40
Ice cream = $1.20
Milkshake = $2.20

1) What is the total cost of a Chips, a Milkshake, and a Cheeseburger?

2) If Alice wanted to buy a Hamburger and a Cheeseburger, how much money would she need?

3) If George wanted to buy a Cheeseburger, a Ice cream, and a Milkshake, how much would it cost him?

4) Billy wants to buy a Ice cream, a Hamburger, and a Hot dog. How much will he have to pay?

5) If Anish wanted to buy a Cola and a Hamburger, how much would he have to pay?

6) Rory purchases a Milkshake, a Ice cream, and a Cola. How much change will he get back from $10.00?

7) If Allan buys a Milkshake and a Hamburger, how much change will he get back from $10.00?

8) What is the total cost of a Hot dog?

9) Paul purchases a Cola and a Milkshake. How much money will he get back if he pays $10.00?

10) Brian wants to buy a Cola, a Milkshake, and a Ice cream. How much money will he need?

A. $4.80   B. $6.40   C. $5.30   D. $5.90   E. $5.20   F. $3.90   G. $1.30

H. $6.80   I. $5.00   J. $6.90

Score: /10

68

What Time is it?

Write the time in the box underneath the clock.

1)

2)

3)

4)

What Time is it?

write on the clock hands.

1)

11:20

2)

3:50

3)

4:30

4)

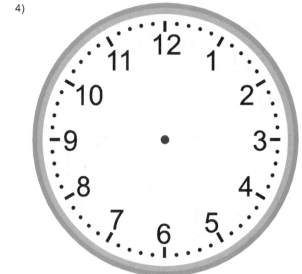

11:00

Draw the clock hands to show the passage of time.

1)

What time will it be in 2 hours 10 minutes?

2)

What time will it be in 4 hours 0 minutes?

What Time Was It?

Draw the clock hands to show the passage of time.

1)

What time was it 1 hour 0 minutes ago?

2)

What time was it 1 hour 10 minutes ago?

a) Zeeshan fills the jug 3/4 of the way up with water. What volume is in the jug?

_____

b) He then pours 500 ml away. How much is left?

_____

c) He then doubles the amount of remaining water. How much water is in the jug now?

_____

Money as Words

Express the currency values in words.

1) **$25.15** ....

2) **$92.87** ....

3) **$64.14** ....

4) **$80.14** ....

5) **$38.72** ....

6) **$92.09** ....

7) **$73.05** ....

8) **$20.78** ....

9) **$77.97** ....

10) **$95.13** ....

Score: /10

Words as Money

Express these sentences as currency values.

1) .... **sixteen dollars sixty cents**

2) .... **twenty-six dollars zero cents**

3) .... **ninety-eight dollars forty-six cents**

4) .... **twelve dollars fifty-five cents**

5) .... **fourteen dollars ninety-one cents**

6) .... **thirteen dollars forty-two cents**

7) .... **thirty dollars thirteen cents**

8) .... **seven dollars thirteen cents**

9) .... **forty-nine dollars sixty-eight cents**

10) .... **ninety-nine dollars eighty-eight cents**

Score: /10

Section 6: Geometry

Name: _____ Date: _____

Class: _____ Teacher: _____

Name the Shape

1)

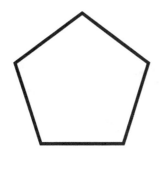

----

2)

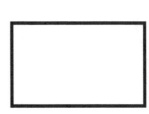

----

3)

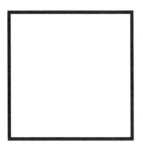

----

4)

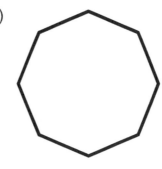

----

5)

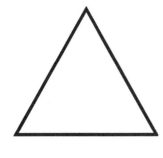

----

6)

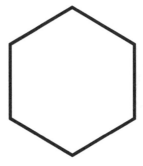

Score: /6

Name the Shape 2

1)

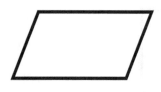

----

2)

----

3)

----

4)

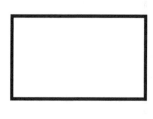

----

5)

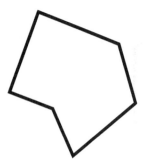

----

6)

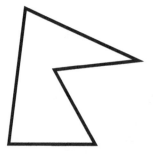

Score: /6

Circle the pentagons.

1)

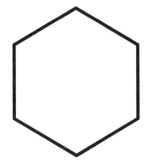

2)

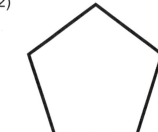

3)

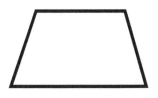

4)

5)

6)

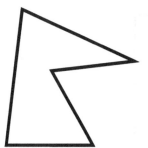

Score: /6

Spotting Hexagons

Circle the hexagons.

1)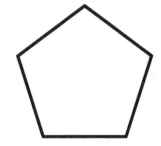

2)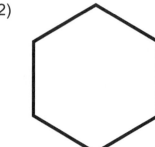

3)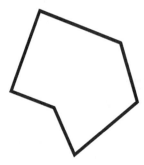

4)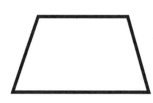

5)

6)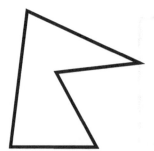

Score: /6

Add in the shapes to complete the pattern.

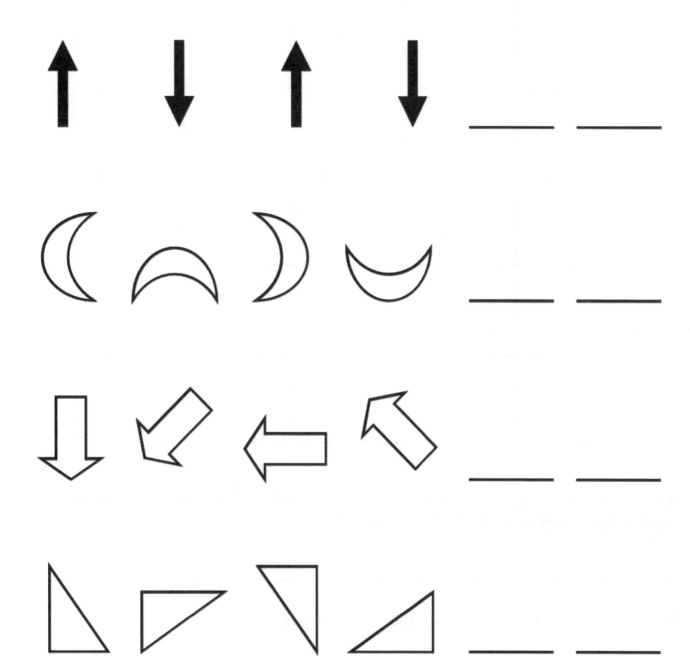

Score: _____ /4

Help Charlie Get Home!

Show Charlie the direction home.

a) Charlie moves two squares up and two squares right to get home to the pond. Is this correct?

_____

b) How far should Charlie have moved?

_____

c) From the original position Charlie makes a quarter turn to the right and moves forward three squares. Draw on the quickest way home now.

_____

Section 7: Statistics

Name: _____   Date: _____

Class: _____   Teacher: _____

Complete the Pictogram

Complete the pictogram using the data provided.

Animals	Tally
Giraffes	|||
Elephants	⊬⊬⊬
Rhinos	||
Lions	⊬⊬⊬

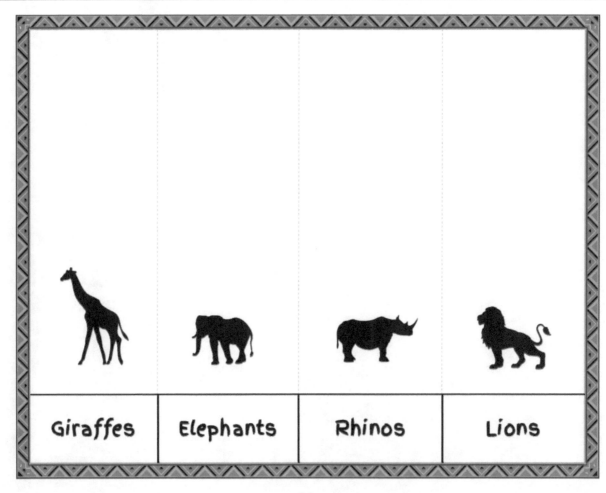

| Giraffes | Elephants | Rhinos | Lions |

Here is a tally chart for a group's favorite animals.

Animal	Tally	Total
Crocodile	卌	
Elephant	卌 IIII	
Rhino	IIII	
Tiger	卌 II	

a) Write in the totals for all the animals.

_____

b) Which animal is the most popular and which is the least popular?

_____

c) How many more votes would the second most popular animal need to have the most votes?

_____

Tally Chart 2

Finish the tally chart for a classroom's favorite colors.

Color	Tally	Total
Red		7
Blue		9
Green		10
Yellow		5

a) Write in the tally numbers for all the colors.

b) How many students were in the class?

c) Did more students like red or blue or did more students like green or yellow? Show your working.

Bar Charts

This bar chart shows the fruit for sale at a supermarket.

1)

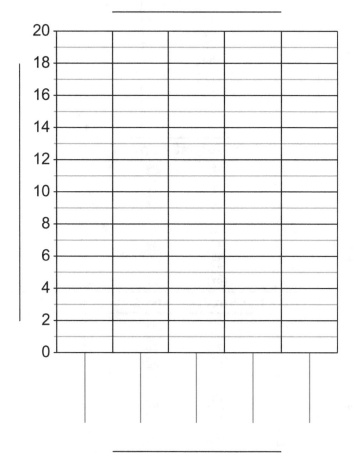

Supermarket Fruit

Fruit	Quantity
Peaches	2
Apples	10
Pears	18
Oranges	20
Plums	14

a) Complete the bar chart adding in the graph title, axis titles and bars.

_____

b) Which fruit does the supermarket have most in stock?

_____

c) Which fruit does the supermarket have the least in stock?

_____

ANSWERS

Section 1

Counting on a Line

1) 60, 35, 80, 25

2) 65, 25, 20, 90

3) 30, 55, 90, 10

4) 30, 70, 75, 90

5) 70, 15, 20, 35

6) 90, 35, 5, 40

1) 35, 75, 60, 45

2) 90, 5, 95, 60

3) 70, 65, 95, 90

4) 25, 90, 40, 35

5) 95, 85, 5, 75

6) 65, 40, 90, 5

Before and After

1) 33 34 35 2) 93 94 95 3) 84 85 86 4) 35 36 37
5) 12 13 14 6) 51 52 53 7) 39 40 41 8) 25 26 27
9) 22 23 24 10) 27 28 29 11) 63 64 65 12) 52 53 54
13) 78 79 80 14) 41 42 43 15) 74 75 76 16) 34 35 36

Circle the Smallest Numbers

1) 67	2) (15)	3) (18)	4) 45	5) 93
81	19	23	(40)	52
(6)	99	57	78	(21)
86	27	61	43	67
93	86	65	93	40
6) 57	7) 63	8) (1)	9) 74	10) 30
26	56	6	83	90
(5)	58	20	(3)	66
66	(13)	82	16	(34)
20	72	27	43	(21)

Circle the Biggest Numbers

1) 46	2) 15	3) (89)	4) 61	5) 39
(65)	(60)	13	64	19
23	38	32	43	(95)
9	45	7	(89)	16
22	36	23	63	10
6) 48	7) 59	8) 32	9) 68	10) 50
5	71	49	(74)	(96)
24	45	(90)	46	93
9	73	57	37	81
(66)	(97)	41	60	66

Circle the Smallest and Biggest Numbers

1) 3	2) 86	3) 32	4) 89	5) (92)
(99)	52	(85)	71	73
36	71	26	(91)	23
(0)	(49)	(15)	41	(0)
73	(92)	68	(8)	67
6) (99)	7) 64	8) 17	9) (85)	10) 50
(26)	(85)	63	68	41
39	43	27	73	25
71	20	(87)	(39)	(95)
64	(8)	(0)	69	(24)

Circle the Odd Numbers

1) (73)	2) 76	3) 12	4) (41)	5) 8
10	(35)	(99)	(5)	64
4	(33)	84	94	54
(17)	74	(27)	60	6
(29)	60	(47)	(71)	(5)
6) 50	7) 14	8) 38	9) 30	10) (83)
60	(75)	2	52	(45)
98	40	90	(27)	92
48	(91)	32	(87)	(27)
84	74	(81)	(85)	44

Circle the Even Numbers

1) (46)	2) (56)	3) (74)	4) (24)	5) 3
(64)	(96)	35	(44)	(4)
(24)	(10)	25	(36)	(28)
(16)	(24)	75	(72)	89
(8)	(26)	97	3	77
6) 11	7) (68)	8) 51	9) 91	10) 27
27	(70)	23	65	51
(20)	3	(82)	5	89
21	(38)	(18)	(6)	61
(4)	(50)	(42)	95	39

Numbers as Words

1) 17 seventeen
2) 11 eleven
3) 12 twelve
4) 15 fifteen
5) 16 sixteen
6) 6 six
7) 13 thirteen
8) 19 nineteen
9) 9 nine
10) 5 five

Words as Numbers

1) 16 sixteen
2) 19 nineteen
3) 20 twenty
4) 11 eleven
5) 6 six
6) 7 seven
7) 15 fifteen
8) 8 eight
9) 12 twelve
10) 18 eighteen

Place Values

1) 98 = 9 tens
2) 1 = 1 one
3) 22 = 2 tens
4) 49 = 4 tens
5) 13 = 1 ten
6) 37 = 7 ones
7) 5 = 5 ones
8) 44 = 4 tens
9) 53 = 5 tens
10) 63 = 6 tens
11) 45 = 4 tens
12) 29 = 2 tens

Number Comparison

1) 25 < 91
2) 1 < 65
3) 3 < 74
4) 21 > 6
5) 5 > 4
6) 18 > 2
7) 4 < 95
8) 42 > 1
9) 33 < 75
10) 5 = 5

Number Lines

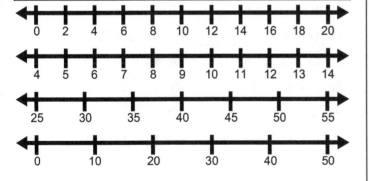

Order the Numbers

1)
19	17
71	19
76	71
85	76
17	82
82	85

2)
44	37
73	44
37	45
45	53
86	73
53	86

3)
91	17
63	18
44	41
17	44
41	63
18	91

Fill in the Missing Numbers

| 20 | 25 | 30 | 35 | 40 | 45 | 50 | 55 | 60 | 65 |

| 16 | 18 | 20 | 22 | 24 | 26 | 28 | 30 | 32 | 34 |

| 75 | 72 | 69 | 66 | 63 | 60 | 57 | 54 | 51 | 48 |

| 90 | 80 | 70 | 60 | 50 | 40 | 30 | 20 | 10 | 0 |

| 75 | 70 | 65 | 60 | 55 | 50 | 45 | 40 | 35 | 30 |

| 5 | 10 | 15 | 20 | 25 | 30 | 35 | 40 | 45 | 50 |

| 10 | 20 | 30 | 40 | 50 | 60 | 70 | 80 | 90 | 100 |

| 82 | 80 | 78 | 76 | 74 | 72 | 70 | 68 | 66 | 64 |

| 20 | 25 | 30 | 35 | 40 | 45 | 50 | 55 | 60 | 65 |

| 48 | 50 | 52 | 54 | 56 | 58 | 60 | 62 | 64 | 66 |

Section 2

Pictorial Addition

1) ✿✿✿✿✿✿ + ✿✿✿✿✿ ✿ = $\boxed{11}$

2) 🍁🍁🍁🍁🍁 + 🍁🍁🍁🍁 🍁🍁🍁 = $\boxed{13}$

3) ✺✺✺✺✺ ✺✺✺✺ + ✺✺✺✺✺ ✺ = $\boxed{15}$

4) ☼☼☼☼☼ + ☼☼☼☼☼ ☼☼ = $\boxed{12}$

5) ♥♥♥♥♥ ♥♥ + ♥♥♥♥♥ ♥♥ = $\boxed{14}$

Part-whole Models

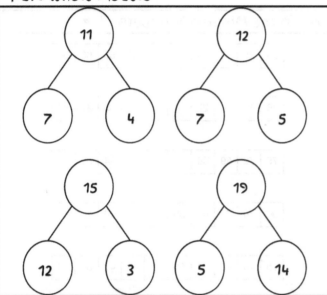

Adding Toucans

8 toucans.

Adding 3 Single Digits

1)	2)	3)	4)	5)
3	7	1	6	7
1	9	3	2	4
+ 2	+ 5	+ 4	+ 7	+ 8
6	21	8	15	19

6)	7)	8)	9)	10)
1	9	9	5	7
6	5	4	4	2
+ 9	+ 8	+ 8	+ 5	+ 4
16	22	21	14	13

11)	12)	13)	14)	15)
8	9	9	1	9
5	6	8	7	6
+ 6	+ 9	+ 5	+ 3	+ 4
19	24	22	11	19

Fact Families

1)
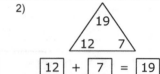

$\boxed{10}$ + $\boxed{13}$ = $\boxed{23}$

$\boxed{13}$ + $\boxed{10}$ = $\boxed{23}$

$\boxed{23}$ - $\boxed{10}$ = $\boxed{13}$

$\boxed{23}$ - $\boxed{13}$ = $\boxed{10}$

2)

$\boxed{12}$ + $\boxed{7}$ = $\boxed{19}$

$\boxed{7}$ + $\boxed{12}$ = $\boxed{19}$

$\boxed{19}$ - $\boxed{12}$ = $\boxed{7}$

$\boxed{19}$ - $\boxed{7}$ = $\boxed{12}$

3)

$\boxed{13}$ + $\boxed{1}$ = $\boxed{14}$

$\boxed{1}$ + $\boxed{13}$ = $\boxed{14}$

$\boxed{14}$ - $\boxed{13}$ = $\boxed{1}$

$\boxed{14}$ - $\boxed{1}$ = $\boxed{13}$

4)

$\boxed{5}$ + $\boxed{16}$ = $\boxed{21}$

$\boxed{16}$ + $\boxed{5}$ = $\boxed{21}$

$\boxed{21}$ - $\boxed{5}$ = $\boxed{16}$

$\boxed{21}$ - $\boxed{16}$ = $\boxed{5}$

Written Questions

a) 89

b) 83

c) 25

d) 43

e) 25

f) 41

Mixed Operations 0-20: Part 1

1) 4 - 2 = 2

2) 7 - 6 = 1

3) 12 - 4 = 8

4) 5 - 3 = 2

5) 14 + 4 = 18

6) 19 + 15 = 34

7) 2 + 9 = 11

8) 14 - 4 = 10

9) 14 + 1 = 15

10) 8 - 6 = 2

11) 8 + 12 = 20

12) 19 - 13 = 6

13) 4 + 6 = 10

14) 13 - 10 = 3

15) 14 + 2 = 16

16) 10 + 16 = 26

17) 6 + 5 = 11

18) 19 + 1 = 20

19) 14 - 8 = 6

20) 17 - 13 = 4

Mixed Operations 0-20: Part 2

1) $4 + 5 = 9$	2) $10 - 4 = 6$	3) $5 - 3 = 2$	4) $8 - 5 = 3$	5) $9 - 4 = 5$
6) $11 + 18 = 29$	7) $4 + 14 = 18$	8) $7 + 2 = 9$	9) $5 + 9 = 14$	10) $16 - 14 = 2$
11) $17 - 0 = 17$	12) $17 + 4 = 21$	13) $12 + 6 = 18$	14) $19 - 16 = 3$	15) $11 - 2 = 9$
16) $19 + 17 = 36$	17) $7 - 0 = 7$	18) $2 - 1 = 1$	19) $12 - 6 = 6$	20) $3 + 8 = 11$
21) $15 + 5 = 20$	22) $18 - 8 = 10$	23) $2 + 12 = 14$	24) $15 + 13 = 28$	25) $9 + 18 = 27$
26) $6 - 0 = 6$	27) $12 + 5 = 17$	28) $3 - 1 = 2$	29) $14 - 13 = 1$	30) $19 + 11 = 30$

Charlie Croc!

Left side: 62

Right side: 46

$30 + 29 + 17 = 76$

Adding Numbers 0-100: Part 1

1) $16 + 40 = 56$	2) $41 + 30 = 71$	3) $21 + 50 = 71$	4) $19 + 30 = 49$	5) $6 + 20 = 26$
6) $7 + 50 = 57$	7) $17 + 40 = 57$	8) $9 + 30 = 39$	9) $41 + 20 = 61$	10) $41 + 10 = 51$
11) $17 + 20 = 37$	12) $6 + 50 = 56$	13) $44 + 50 = 94$	14) $12 + 60 = 72$	15) $15 + 60 = 75$
16) $32 + 50 = 82$	17) $49 + 30 = 79$	18) $11 + 40 = 51$	19) $11 + 20 = 31$	20) $13 + 60 = 73$

Adding Numbers 0-100: Part 2

1) $41 + 12 = 53$	2) $47 + 31 = 78$	3) $48 + 27 = 75$	4) $41 + 56 = 97$	5) $48 + 35 = 83$
6) $52 + 29 = 81$	7) $60 + 22 = 82$	8) $31 + 41 = 72$	9) $64 + 21 = 85$	10) $37 + 43 = 80$
11) $31 + 62 = 93$	12) $52 + 43 = 95$	13) $53 + 46 = 99$	14) $31 + 56 = 87$	15) $42 + 46 = 88$
16) $31 + 69 = 100$	17) $40 + 42 = 82$	18) $45 + 37 = 82$	19) $51 + 41 = 92$	20) $59 + 11 = 70$

Subtracting Numbers 0-100

1) $79 - 41 = 38$	2) $61 - 6 = 55$	3) $65 - 5 = 60$	4) $56 - 25 = 31$	5) $75 - 19 = 56$
6) $80 - 11 = 69$	7) $89 - 10 = 79$	8) $58 - 5 = 53$	9) $94 - 45 = 49$	10) $60 - 35 = 25$
11) $60 - 42 = 18$	12) $99 - 32 = 67$	13) $88 - 39 = 49$	14) $81 - 31 = 50$	15) $83 - 4 = 79$
16) $82 - 15 = 67$	17) $86 - 48 = 38$	18) $65 - 28 = 37$	19) $58 - 10 = 48$	20) $79 - 16 = 63$

Mixed Operations 0-100

1) $12 + 21 = 33$	2) $55 + 44 = 99$	3) $0 + 24 = 24$	4) $23 - 12 = 11$	5) $14 + 32 = 46$
6) $50 - 39 = 11$	7) $54 - 30 = 24$	8) $62 - 28 = 34$	9) $42 - 5 = 37$	10) $7 - 4 = 3$
11) $38 - 7 = 31$	12) $10 + 36 = 46$	13) $23 + 3 = 26$	14) $21 + 17 = 38$	15) $61 - 33 = 28$
16) $8 - 6 = 2$	17) $44 - 10 = 34$	18) $17 - 9 = 8$	19) $67 - 29 = 38$	20) $9 - 4 = 5$
21) $56 - 23 = 33$	22) $22 - 19 = 3$	23) $33 + 9 = 42$	24) $14 + 56 = 70$	25) $30 + 1 = 31$
26) $44 + 1 = 45$	27) $14 + 31 = 45$	28) $1 + 42 = 43$	29) $7 + 21 = 28$	30) $10 + 47 = 57$

Section 3

Multiplying by 2: Part 1

1) $8 \times 2 = 16$	2) $7 \times 2 = 14$	3) $5 \times 2 = 10$
4) $2 \times 2 = 4$	5) $6 \times 2 = 12$	6) $3 \times 2 = 6$
7) $9 \times 2 = 18$	8) $1 \times 2 = 2$	9) $4 \times 2 = 8$
10) $7 \times 2 = 14$	11) $1 \times 2 = 2$	12) $8 \times 2 = 16$
13) $7 \times 2 = 14$	14) $2 \times 2 = 4$	15) $7 \times 2 = 14$
16) $6 \times 2 = 12$	17) $6 \times 2 = 12$	18) $3 \times 2 = 6$
19) $5 \times 2 = 10$	20) $3 \times 2 = 6$	21) $8 \times 2 = 16$
22) $7 \times 2 = 14$	23) $7 \times 2 = 14$	24) $6 \times 2 = 12$
25) $2 \times 2 = 4$	26) $6 \times 2 = 12$	27) $4 \times 2 = 8$
28) $5 \times 2 = 10$	29) $5 \times 2 = 10$	30) $2 \times 2 = 4$

Multiplying by 2: Part 2

1) $2 \times 5 = 10$	2) $2 \times 3 = 6$	3) $2 \times 4 = 8$
4) $2 \times 8 = 16$	5) $2 \times 9 = 18$	6) $2 \times 7 = 14$
7) $2 \times 2 = 4$	8) $2 \times 6 = 12$	9) $2 \times 1 = 2$
10) $2 \times 4 = 8$	11) $2 \times 7 = 14$	12) $2 \times 9 = 18$
13) $2 \times 6 = 12$	14) $2 \times 6 = 12$	15) $2 \times 2 = 4$
16) $2 \times 3 = 6$	17) $2 \times 1 = 2$	18) $2 \times 8 = 16$
19) $2 \times 6 = 12$	20) $2 \times 7 = 14$	21) $2 \times 5 = 10$
22) $2 \times 2 = 4$	23) $2 \times 3 = 6$	24) $2 \times 7 = 14$
25) $2 \times 6 = 12$	26) $2 \times 7 = 14$	27) $2 \times 1 = 2$
28) $2 \times 1 = 2$	29) $2 \times 1 = 2$	30) $2 \times 4 = 8$

Multiplying by 5: Part 1

1) $5 \times 5 = 25$	2) $1 \times 5 = 5$	3) $8 \times 5 = 40$
4) $6 \times 5 = 30$	5) $9 \times 5 = 45$	6) $3 \times 5 = 15$
7) $7 \times 5 = 35$	8) $4 \times 5 = 20$	9) $2 \times 5 = 10$
10) $3 \times 5 = 15$	11) $5 \times 5 = 25$	12) $5 \times 5 = 25$
13) $2 \times 5 = 10$	14) $3 \times 5 = 15$	15) $6 \times 5 = 30$
16) $8 \times 5 = 40$	17) $4 \times 5 = 20$	18) $6 \times 5 = 30$
19) $6 \times 5 = 30$	20) $3 \times 5 = 15$	21) $9 \times 5 = 45$
22) $9 \times 5 = 45$	23) $9 \times 5 = 45$	24) $2 \times 5 = 10$
25) $3 \times 5 = 15$	26) $3 \times 5 = 15$	27) $7 \times 5 = 35$
28) $4 \times 5 = 20$	29) $4 \times 5 = 20$	30) $7 \times 5 = 35$

Multiplying by 5: Part 2

1) $5 \times 1 = 5$	2) $5 \times 6 = 30$	3) $5 \times 2 = 10$
4) $5 \times 5 = 25$	5) $5 \times 7 = 35$	6) $5 \times 3 = 15$
7) $5 \times 8 = 40$	8) $5 \times 4 = 20$	9) $5 \times 9 = 45$
10) $5 \times 1 = 5$	11) $5 \times 6 = 30$	12) $5 \times 3 = 15$
13) $5 \times 3 = 15$	14) $5 \times 2 = 10$	15) $5 \times 1 = 5$
16) $5 \times 5 = 25$	17) $5 \times 2 = 10$	18) $5 \times 5 = 25$
19) $5 \times 3 = 15$	20) $5 \times 9 = 45$	21) $5 \times 7 = 35$
22) $5 \times 8 = 40$	23) $5 \times 1 = 5$	24) $5 \times 9 = 45$
25) $5 \times 5 = 25$	26) $5 \times 2 = 10$	27) $5 \times 3 = 15$
28) $5 \times 3 = 15$	29) $5 \times 6 = 30$	30) $5 \times 5 = 25$

Multiplying by 10: Part 1

1) $8 \times 10 = 80$	2) $1 \times 10 = 10$	3) $6 \times 10 = 60$
4) $7 \times 10 = 70$	5) $3 \times 10 = 30$	6) $4 \times 10 = 40$
7) $9 \times 10 = 90$	8) $5 \times 10 = 50$	9) $2 \times 10 = 20$
10) $6 \times 10 = 60$	11) $7 \times 10 = 70$	12) $7 \times 10 = 70$
13) $3 \times 10 = 30$	14) $9 \times 10 = 90$	15) $5 \times 10 = 50$
16) $5 \times 10 = 50$	17) $2 \times 10 = 20$	18) $4 \times 10 = 40$
19) $3 \times 10 = 30$	20) $1 \times 10 = 10$	21) $8 \times 10 = 80$
22) $2 \times 10 = 20$	23) $6 \times 10 = 60$	24) $3 \times 10 = 30$
25) $2 \times 10 = 20$	26) $8 \times 10 = 80$	27) $6 \times 10 = 60$
28) $5 \times 10 = 50$	29) $4 \times 10 = 40$	30) $5 \times 10 = 50$

Multiplying by 10: Part 2

1) $10 \times 8 = 80$	2) $10 \times 7 = 70$	3) $10 \times 2 = 20$
4) $10 \times 6 = 60$	5) $10 \times 5 = 50$	6) $10 \times 4 = 40$
7) $10 \times 9 = 90$	8) $10 \times 3 = 30$	9) $10 \times 1 = 10$
10) $10 \times 5 = 50$	11) $10 \times 6 = 60$	12) $10 \times 3 = 30$
13) $10 \times 2 = 20$	14) $10 \times 7 = 70$	15) $10 \times 2 = 20$
16) $10 \times 7 = 70$	17) $10 \times 4 = 40$	18) $10 \times 3 = 30$
19) $10 \times 3 = 30$	20) $10 \times 7 = 70$	21) $10 \times 7 = 70$
22) $10 \times 5 = 50$	23) $10 \times 2 = 20$	24) $10 \times 2 = 20$
25) $10 \times 5 = 50$	26) $10 \times 8 = 80$	27) $10 \times 7 = 70$
28) $10 \times 5 = 50$	29) $10 \times 8 = 80$	30) $10 \times 4 = 40$

Right or wrong?

The following sums are incorrect:

$2 \times 1 = 4$

$5 \div 4 = 12$

$100 \div 10 = 1$

$2 \div 2 = 2$

Multiplication Patterns

1) Count by 12 from 0 to 108

0	12	24	36	48	60	72	84	96	108

2) Count by 1 from 0 to 9

0	1	2	3	4	5	6	7	8	9

3) Count by 6 from 0 to 54

0	6	12	18	24	30	36	42	48	54

4) Count by 8 from 0 to 72

0	8	16	24	32	40	48	56	64	72

5) Count by 7 from 0 to 63

0	7	14	21	28	35	42	49	56	63

6) Count by 4 from 0 to 36

0	4	8	12	16	20	24	28	32	36

7) Count by 5 from 0 to 45

0	5	10	15	20	25	30	35	40	45

8) Count by 11 from 0 to 99

0	11	22	33	44	55	66	77	88	99

Word Problems: Multiplication

1) 6 2) 12 3) 2 4) 16 5) 6

Dividing by 2

1) $56 \div 2 = 28$	2) $80 \div 2 = 40$
3) $50 \div 2 = 25$	4) $14 \div 2 = 7$
5) $36 \div 2 = 18$	6) $78 \div 2 = 39$
7) $92 \div 2 = 46$	8) $10 \div 2 = 5$
9) $96 \div 2 = 48$	10) $4 \div 2 = 2$
11) $12 \div 2 = 6$	12) $100 \div 2 = 50$
13) $76 \div 2 = 38$	14) $38 \div 2 = 19$
15) $72 \div 2 = 36$	16) $26 \div 2 = 13$
17) $34 \div 2 = 17$	18) $52 \div 2 = 26$
19) $74 \div 2 = 37$	20) $18 \div 2 = 9$
21) $28 \div 2 = 14$	22) $68 \div 2 = 34$
23) $84 \div 2 = 42$	24) $86 \div 2 = 43$
25) $32 \div 2 = 16$	26) $24 \div 2 = 12$
27) $16 \div 2 = 8$	28) $46 \div 2 = 23$
29) $20 \div 2 = 10$	30) $30 \div 2 = 15$

Dividing by 5

1) $40 \div 5 = 8$	2) $45 \div 5 = 9$
3) $80 \div 5 = 16$	4) $10 \div 5 = 2$
5) $55 \div 5 = 11$	6) $15 \div 5 = 3$
7) $50 \div 5 = 10$	8) $25 \div 5 = 5$
9) $100 \div 5 = 20$	10) $30 \div 5 = 6$
11) $85 \div 5 = 17$	12) $60 \div 5 = 12$
13) $20 \div 5 = 4$	14) $5 \div 5 = 1$
15) $70 \div 5 = 14$	16) $75 \div 5 = 15$
17) $65 \div 5 = 13$	18) $95 \div 5 = 19$
19) $35 \div 5 = 7$	20) $90 \div 5 = 18$
21) $95 \div 5 = 19$	22) $25 \div 5 = 5$
23) $30 \div 5 = 6$	24) $20 \div 5 = 4$
25) $5 \div 5 = 1$	26) $55 \div 5 = 11$
27) $50 \div 5 = 10$	28) $40 \div 5 = 8$
29) $40 \div 5 = 8$	30) $65 \div 5 = 13$

Dividing by 10

1) $90 \div 10 = 9$	2) $50 \div 10 = 5$
3) $40 \div 10 = 4$	4) $60 \div 10 = 6$
5) $20 \div 10 = 2$	6) $10 \div 10 = 1$
7) $80 \div 10 = 8$	8) $70 \div 10 = 7$
9) $100 \div 10 = 10$	10) $30 \div 10 = 3$
11) $80 \div 10 = 8$	12) $80 \div 10 = 8$
13) $100 \div 10 = 10$	14) $30 \div 10 = 3$
15) $80 \div 10 = 8$	16) $70 \div 10 = 7$
17) $20 \div 10 = 2$	18) $60 \div 10 = 6$
19) $70 \div 10 = 7$	20) $40 \div 10 = 4$

Word Problems: Division

1) 2 2) 4 3) 5 4) 5 5) 3

Table Drill

1)

✖	10	7	11	8	5
8	80	56	88	64	40
10	100	70	110	80	50
3	30	21	33	24	15
7	70	49	77	56	35
0	0	0	0	0	0

2)

✖	3	1	9	8	5
1	3	1	9	8	5
4	12	4	36	32	20
3	9	3	27	24	15
5	15	5	45	40	25
11	33	11	99	88	55

3)

✖	4	12	7	2	11
7	28	84	49	14	77
10	40	120	70	20	110
3	12	36	21	6	33
5	20	60	35	10	55
0	0	0	0	0	0

4)

✖	8	3	12	6	7
10	80	30	120	60	70
5	40	15	60	30	35
12	96	36	144	72	84
4	32	12	48	24	28
3	24	9	36	18	21

Fact Families

1)

3	$\times$	9	$= 27$
9	$\times$	3	$= 27$
27	$\div$	3	$= 9$
27	$\div$	9	$= 3$

2)

9	$\times$	5	$= 45$
5	$\times$	9	$= 45$
45	$\div$	9	$= 5$
45	$\div$	5	$= 9$

3)

5	$\times$	9	$= 45$
9	$\times$	5	$= 45$
45	$\div$	5	$= 9$
45	$\div$	9	$= 5$

4)

10	$\times$	7	$= 70$
7	$\times$	10	$= 70$
70	$\div$	10	$= 7$
70	$\div$	7	$= 10$

The Maze!

From the left:

$7 \times 4 = 28$
$7 \times 1 = 7$
$8 \div 2 = 4$
$5 \times 8 = 40$
$14 \div 7 = 2$
$3 \times 8 = 24$
$7 \times 9 = 63$
$8 \times 10 = 80$

Section 4

Shading Shapes

a) 8
b) Shade in any single, individual square.
c) Shade in any combination of 3 out of 4 squares.

Shade the Fraction

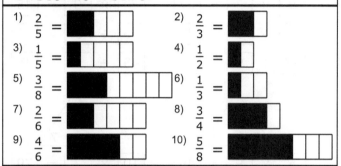

1) $\frac{2}{5} =$
2) $\frac{2}{3} =$
3) $\frac{1}{5} =$
4) $\frac{1}{2} =$
5) $\frac{3}{8} =$
6) $\frac{1}{3} =$
7) $\frac{2}{6} =$
8) $\frac{3}{4} =$
9) $\frac{4}{6} =$
10) $\frac{5}{8} =$

Identify the Shaded Fraction

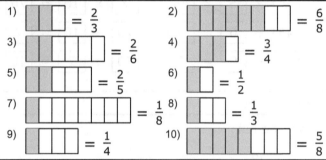

1) $= \frac{2}{3}$
2) $= \frac{6}{8}$
3) $= \frac{2}{6}$
4) $= \frac{3}{4}$
5) $= \frac{2}{5}$
6) $= \frac{1}{2}$
7) $= \frac{1}{8}$
8) $= \frac{1}{3}$
9) $= \frac{1}{4}$
10) $= \frac{5}{8}$

Charlie's Pizza

a) Initially Charlie eats 1/4 (a quarter) of the pizza.
b) He then eats 1/2 more. So he is now left with a 1/4 of his pizza.

Fractions on a Line

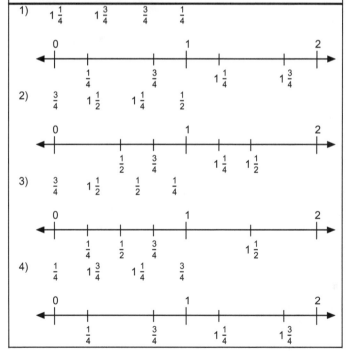

1) $1\frac{1}{4}$ $1\frac{3}{4}$ $\frac{3}{4}$ $\frac{1}{4}$

2) $\frac{3}{4}$ $1\frac{1}{2}$ $1\frac{1}{4}$ $\frac{1}{2}$

3) $\frac{3}{4}$ $1\frac{1}{2}$ $\frac{1}{2}$ $\frac{1}{4}$

4) $\frac{1}{4}$ $1\frac{3}{4}$ $1\frac{1}{4}$ $\frac{3}{4}$

Add the Fractions

1) $\begin{array}{r} \frac{2}{4} \\ + \frac{3}{4} \\ \hline \frac{5}{4} \end{array}$
2) $\begin{array}{r} \frac{1}{3} \\ + \frac{2}{3} \\ \hline \frac{1}{1} \end{array}$
3) $\begin{array}{r} \frac{4}{5} \\ + \frac{4}{5} \\ \hline \frac{8}{5} \end{array}$
4) $\begin{array}{r} \frac{4}{6} \\ + \frac{1}{6} \\ \hline \frac{5}{6} \end{array}$
5) $\begin{array}{r} \frac{1}{2} \\ + \frac{1}{2} \\ \hline \frac{1}{1} \end{array}$

6) $\begin{array}{r} \frac{2}{4} \\ + \frac{1}{4} \\ \hline \frac{3}{4} \end{array}$
7) $\begin{array}{r} \frac{2}{5} \\ + \frac{4}{5} \\ \hline \frac{6}{5} \end{array}$
8) $\begin{array}{r} \frac{2}{3} \\ + \frac{2}{3} \\ \hline \frac{4}{3} \end{array}$
9) $\begin{array}{r} \frac{1}{4} \\ + \frac{1}{4} \\ \hline \frac{1}{2} \end{array}$
10) $\begin{array}{r} \frac{2}{3} \\ + \frac{1}{3} \\ \hline \frac{1}{1} \end{array}$

11) $\begin{array}{r} \frac{2}{5} \\ + \frac{3}{5} \\ \hline \frac{1}{1} \end{array}$
12) $\begin{array}{r} \frac{1}{6} \\ + \frac{1}{6} \\ \hline \frac{1}{3} \end{array}$
13) $\begin{array}{r} \frac{3}{4} \\ + \frac{1}{4} \\ \hline \frac{1}{1} \end{array}$
14) $\begin{array}{r} \frac{3}{6} \\ + \frac{1}{6} \\ \hline \frac{2}{3} \end{array}$
15) $\begin{array}{r} \frac{3}{5} \\ + \frac{4}{5} \\ \hline \frac{7}{5} \end{array}$

16) $\begin{array}{r} \frac{3}{6} \\ + \frac{5}{6} \\ \hline \frac{4}{3} \end{array}$
17) $\begin{array}{r} \frac{2}{5} \\ + \frac{1}{5} \\ \hline \frac{3}{5} \end{array}$
18) $\begin{array}{r} \frac{4}{5} \\ + \frac{3}{5} \\ \hline \frac{7}{5} \end{array}$
19) $\begin{array}{r} \frac{5}{6} \\ + \frac{1}{6} \\ \hline \frac{1}{1} \end{array}$
20) $\begin{array}{r} \frac{1}{5} \\ + \frac{4}{5} \\ \hline \frac{1}{1} \end{array}$

Group the Animals

a) There are 3 sets of 3 rhinos.
b) The elephants can be split into:
2 groups of 6
3 groups of 4
4 groups of 3
6 groups of 2.

Simplifying Fractions

1) $\frac{16}{32} = \frac{1}{2}$
2) $\frac{40}{48} = \frac{5}{6}$
3) $\frac{18}{27} = \frac{2}{3}$
4) $\frac{24}{32} = \frac{3}{4}$
5) $\frac{15}{25} = \frac{3}{5}$
6) $\frac{28}{35} = \frac{4}{5}$
7) $\frac{54}{72} = \frac{3}{4}$
8) $\frac{7}{28} = \frac{1}{4}$
9) $\frac{9}{27} = \frac{1}{3}$
10) $\frac{20}{24} = \frac{5}{6}$
11) $\frac{42}{48} = \frac{7}{8}$
12) $\frac{36}{45} = \frac{4}{5}$
13) $\frac{6}{18} = \frac{1}{3}$
14) $\frac{25}{30} = \frac{5}{6}$
15) $\frac{9}{12} = \frac{3}{4}$
16) $\frac{27}{54} = \frac{1}{2}$
17) $\frac{49}{56} = \frac{7}{8}$
18) $\frac{12}{15} = \frac{4}{5}$
19) $\frac{7}{21} = \frac{1}{3}$
20) $\frac{5}{20} = \frac{1}{4}$

Equivalent Fractions

1) $\frac{1}{4} = \frac{8}{32}$
2) $\frac{1}{3} = \frac{6}{18}$
3) $\frac{1}{4} = \frac{5}{20}$
4) $\frac{2}{3} = \frac{8}{12}$
5) $\frac{3}{4} = \frac{6}{8}$
6) $\frac{1}{3} = \frac{2}{6}$
7) $\frac{3}{4} = \frac{9}{12}$
8) $\frac{1}{3} = \frac{7}{21}$
9) $\frac{2}{4} = \frac{20}{40}$
10) $\frac{1}{3} = \frac{9}{27}$
11) $\frac{1}{4} = \frac{4}{16}$
12) $\frac{3}{4} = \frac{27}{36}$
13) $\frac{2}{3} = \frac{20}{30}$
14) $\frac{2}{4} = \frac{10}{20}$
15) $\frac{2}{4} = \frac{4}{8}$
16) $\frac{2}{3} = \frac{14}{21}$
17) $\frac{2}{4} = \frac{18}{36}$
18) $\frac{1}{4} = \frac{6}{24}$
19) $\frac{2}{4} = \frac{16}{32}$
20) $\frac{1}{4} = \frac{3}{12}$

Comparing Fractions

1) $\frac{2}{8} < \frac{3}{4}$
2) $\frac{2}{3} > \frac{3}{6}$
3) $\frac{1}{5} < \frac{2}{4}$
4) $\frac{7}{8} > \frac{2}{3}$
5) $\frac{2}{4} > \frac{3}{8}$
6) $\frac{1}{3} < \frac{3}{5}$
7) $\frac{3}{6} = \frac{4}{8}$
8) $\frac{2}{4} < \frac{2}{3}$
9) $\frac{2}{5} < \frac{5}{6}$
10) $\frac{1}{3} < \frac{5}{6}$
11) $\frac{2}{5} < \frac{5}{8}$
12) $\frac{1}{4} < \frac{3}{8}$
13) $\frac{3}{4} > \frac{1}{3}$
14) $\frac{5}{6} > \frac{2}{5}$
15) $\frac{4}{5} > \frac{1}{6}$
16) $\frac{1}{8} < \frac{2}{3}$
17) $\frac{2}{4} = \frac{3}{6}$
18) $\frac{1}{5} < \frac{1}{3}$
19) $\frac{6}{8} > \frac{1}{4}$
20) $\frac{1}{4} < \frac{3}{6}$

Shade the Fractions

1)  $= \frac{3}{5}$

2) 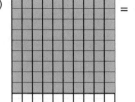 $= \frac{9}{10}$

3)  $= \frac{1}{2}$

4) 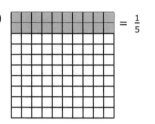 $= \frac{1}{5}$

5) 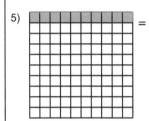 $= \frac{1}{10}$

6) $= \frac{4}{5}$

Translating Fractions to Whole Numbers

1) $\frac{1}{3}$ of 9 = 3

2) $\frac{6}{10}$ of 10 = 6

3) $\frac{3}{8}$ of 8 = 3

4) $\frac{4}{5}$ of 5 = 4

5) $\frac{3}{4}$ of 4 = 3

6) $\frac{6}{8}$ of 8 = 6

7) $\frac{3}{10}$ of 10 = 3

8) $\frac{3}{6}$ of 6 = 3

9) $\frac{1}{2}$ of 8 = 4

10) $\frac{17}{20}$ of 20 = 17

11) $\frac{2}{3}$ of 6 = 4

12) $\frac{1}{2}$ of 6 = 3

13) $\frac{2}{4}$ of 4 = 2

14) $\frac{5}{6}$ of 6 = 5

15) $\frac{1}{10}$ of 10 = 1

16) $\frac{2}{5}$ of 5 = 2

17) $\frac{13}{20}$ of 20 = 13

18) $\frac{5}{8}$ of 8 = 5

19) $\frac{1}{3}$ of 3 = 1

20) $\frac{2}{6}$ of 6 = 2

Identify the Fractions

1)  $= \frac{1}{5}$

2) 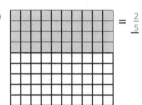 $= \frac{2}{5}$

3) 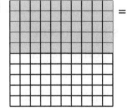 $= \frac{1}{2}$

4) 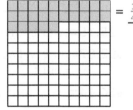 $= \frac{1}{4}$

5) 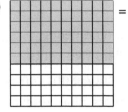 $= \frac{3}{5}$

6) 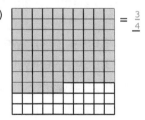 $= \frac{3}{4}$

Section 5

Measuring Lines

a) Line 9 (16cm) is the longest and Line 5 (3cm) is the shortest.

b) 13cm longer.

Gauge the Heat

1) 28°F
2) 26°F
3) 20°F
4) 22°F

1) is the hottest and 3) is the coolest.

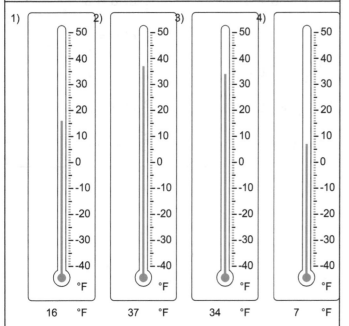

16   °F   37   °F   34   °F   7   °F

b) 2 is the hottest by 3°F

c) 50°F

Shopping Problems

1) $6.90 2) $5.90 3) $6.80 4) $5.00 5) $3.90
6) $5.20 7) $5.30 8) $1.30 9) $6.40
10) $4.80

What Time is it?

1) 4:40

2) 6:10

3) 4:30

4) 8:00

What Time is it?

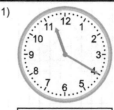   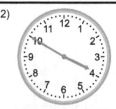

11:20   3:50

   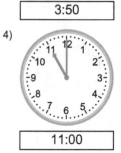

4:30   11:00

What Time will it be?

1)

What time will it
be in 2 hours
10 minutes?

2)

What time will it
be in 4 hours 0
minutes?

What Time was it?

1)

What time was
it 1 hour 0
minutes ago?

2)

What time was
it 1 hour 10
minutes ago?

Measuring Jug

a) 750 ml
b) 250 ml
c) 500 ml

Money as Words

1) $25.15=twenty-five dollars fifteen cents

2) $92.87=ninety-two dollars eighty-seven cents

3) $64.14=sixty-four dollars fourteen cents

4) $80.14=eighty dollars fourteen cents

5) $38.72=thirty-eight dollars seventy-two cents

6) $92.09=ninety-two dollars nine cents

7) $73.05=seventy-three dollars five cents

8) $20.78=twenty dollars seventy-eight cents

9) $77.97=seventy-seven dollars ninety-seven cents

10) $95.13=ninety-five dollars thirteen cents

Words as Money

1) $16.60 = sixteen dollars sixty cents
2) $26.00 = twenty-six dollars zero cents
3) $98.46 = ninety-eight dollars forty-six cents
4) $12.55 = twelve dollars fifty-five cents
5) $14.91 = fourteen dollars ninety-one cents
6) $13.42 = thirteen dollars forty-two cents
7) $30.13 = thirty dollars thirteen cents
8) $7.13 = seven dollars thirteen cents
9) $49.68 = forty-nine dollars sixty-eight cents
10) $99.88 = ninety-nine dollars eighty-eight cents

Section 6

Name the Shape

1) (Regular) Pentagon
2) Rectangle
3) Square
4) (Regular) Octagon
5) (Equilateral) Triangle
6) (Regular) Hexagon

Name the Shape 2

1) Parallelogram
2) (Irregular) Octagon
3) (Isosceles) Triangle
4) Rectangle
5) (Irregular) Hexagon
6) (Irregular) Pentagon

Spotting Pentagons

2) and 6) are pentagons (5 sided).

Spotting Hexagons

2) and 3) are hexagons (6 sided).

Complete the Patterns

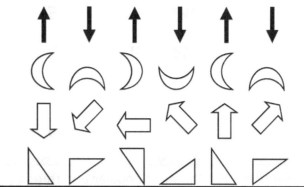

Help Charlie Get Home!

a) Incorrect
b) Charlie should've moved three squares up and three squares right (or three squares right and three squares up).
c) From the new location, Charlie should take a quarter turn left and go three squares up.

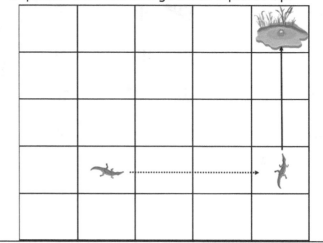

Section 7

Complete the pictogram

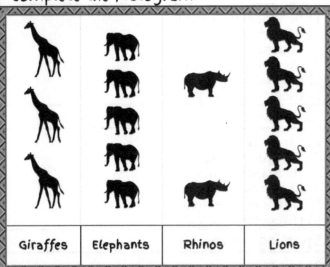

Giraffes	Elephants	Rhinos	Lions

Tally Chart 1

a)

Animal	Tally	Total
Crocodile	卌	5
Elephant	卌 IIII	9
Rhino	IIII	4
Tiger	卌 II	7

b) Elephants are the most popular and rhinos are the least popular.

c) The tiger (7 votes) would need 3 more votes to surpass the elephants (9 votes).

Tally Chart 2

Color	Tally	Total
Red	卌 II	7
Blue	卌 IIII	9
Green	卌 卌	10
Yellow	卌	5

b) There were 31 students in the class.

c) Red (7) + Blue (9) = 16
Green (10) + Yellow (5) = 15.

Therefore, red + blue has more votes.

Bar Charts

a)

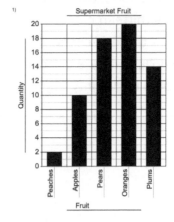

Fruit	Quantity
Peaches	2
Apples	10
Pears	18
Oranges	20
Plums	14

b) Oranges (20) are most in stock.

c) Peaches (2) are least in stock.

Made in United States
Troutdale, OR
11/04/2023

14295925R00058